PENNY WARNER'S
PARTY BOOK

OTHER BOOKS BY PENNY WARNER INCLUDE

Healthy Snacks for Kids

Super Toys

Super Snacks for Kids

Happy Birthday Parties!

A Deadly Game of Klew
(with Tom Warner)

Greetings from the Grave
(with Tom Warner)

The Secret of the Bitter Sweets
(with Tom Warner)

PENNY WARNER'S PARTY BOOK

1001 Tips and Ideas for Hosting the Perfect Party: Wedding and Baby Showers, Birthdays, Anniversaries, Family and School Reunions, Holidays, Housewarmings, "Adults Only," Novelties

PENNY WARNER
Illustrations by CONSTANCE PIKE

ST. MARTIN'S PRESS · NEW YORK

*To the Danville Co-op, indefatigable
partiers.*

PENNY WARNER'S PARTY BOOK. Copyright © 1987 by
Penny Warner. All rights reserved. Printed in the
United States of America. No part of this book may
be used or reproduced in any manner whatsoever
without written permission except in the case of brief
quotations embodied in critical articles or reviews.
For information, address St. Martin's Press, 175 Fifth
Avenue, New York, N.Y. 10010.

Design by Janet Tingey

Library of Congress Cataloging-in-Publication Data

Warner, Penny.
    Penny Warner's party book.

        1. Entertaining.   I. Title.   II. Title: Party book.
GV1471.W27   1987   793.2   87-4442
ISBN 0-312-00666-7 (pbk.)

First Edition
10 9 8 7 6 5 4 3 2 1

ACKNOWLEDGMENTS

Many thanks to Barbara Anderson for the invitation.

And thanks to all my friends who shared their party ideas: Anne Arns, Lynne Bock-Willmes, Dona Bowen, Anne Chalfant, Carolyn Cosetti, Joanne Dahlin, Colleen Dukes, Lucy Galen, Mab Gray, Linda Becky Jenkins, Joan Kramer, Linda Kramer, Julie Lang, Diane Mancher, Connie Pike, Melody Pike, Chris Saunders, Julie Simpson, Gail Pike Sitton, Barbara Swec, Marion Thatch, Melanie Thiele, Doreen Warner, Mary Warner, and Erika Woodrell. Thanks to Stuart Moore and Anne Savarese for all their hard work.

And a special thanks to Rebecca, Matthew, and Tom.

CONTENTS

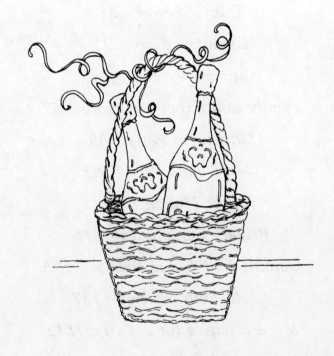

TEN TIPS FOR A PERFECT PARTY

There is only one secret to hosting a perfect party—planning. Follow these ten steps for planning your perfect party.

1. *Plan the type of party you want to have.*

You've decided to have a party. You want to bring together old friends, celebrate a special occasion, or try out a new recipe. Whatever your reason, your party will be more successful and memorable if you build it around a theme. A simple shower, for example, becomes more fun when it's a "toy shower" (for expectant parents) or a "kitchen shower" (for the bride-to-be). You can give a birthday party a theme by making it an "Over-the-Hill" party with a black color scheme or a "Mexican night" with appropriate food and drink. On Valentine's Day, you might make the theme "red" and request that your guests dress in red.

After you've chosen your theme, think about how you'll stage the party. If you've chosen the Academy Awards Party as your theme, perhaps you'd like to make it a formal dinner for a small intimate group. A potluck dinner might be just right for a big Independence Day bash. You may want to host an open house, where the guests wander in and out during an afternoon or evening (a popular type of party during the holidays). Or maybe your party would be best as a luncheon, a brunch, or an afternoon tea, suitable for showers. Stage your party in the park with a picnic, barbecue, or tailgate feast during the football or baseball season. Sometimes a simple party is the best party—just serve appetizers and cocktails or have a dessert marathon. A wine-tasting can be held around almost any theme. And decide whether you want to make it a surprise party—sometimes more work for the host but a lot of fun for the guests.

Have your invitations state the reason, theme, and type of party as well as the mood for the party. Let your guests know how formal or informal it will be so they don't arrive in an uncomfortable mixture of tails and tank tops. Then decorate the party room in keeping with your theme, by transforming your family room into a romantic fantasyland or your patio into a Pacific island. All the games, refreshments, prizes, favors, and gifts should be in keeping with your party theme.

The combinations are limitless—just let your creativity, imagination, and fantasies run free. The decisions are easy once you've decided on the theme.

2. Plan the guest list.

Decide on the size of the party and make out your guest list. Consider the different personalities of your guests and how well they will get along—if some of them are feuding, your party may suffer.

Think about your space in relation to the number of people you're inviting. If the party is outdoors or you have a large room, you'll have no problem with a large party. But if your space is small, you'll have to keep the numbers down to be sure everyone is comfortable.

If it's to be a dinner party, seat each guest next to someone new to help them get acquainted, but don't put the antinuke demonstrator next to the nuclear engineer, unless they're to be the entertainment for the evening. Also, seating your guests alternating man/woman when possible

2

keeps the party more lively and helps prevent it from turning into two separate parties.

3. *Plan your party stages.*

Most parties have definite stages, and if you've planned well for each stage, your party should run smoothly.

The best way to avoid problems during parties is to travel through the party mentally. Just take a few minutes to imagine the guests arriving, the distribution of the food, the flow of the party, the activities planned, and the ending. This way you may foresee some problems that you can correct in advance.

Make sure you have planned for the arrival and introduction of your guests. Party beginnings are usually awkward, and if you remember that the party begins with the first guest, you'll be off to a good start. Then think about when you want to serve refreshments, when to play games, and when to allow free time for socializing.

4. *Plan the food.*

Keep the food simple if you want to enjoy your own party. Finger foods are easy to make, easy to serve, easy to eat, and are best for larger, stand-up parties. Or you might want to try something different, like a serve-yourself salad bar, a dessert contest, or a make-your-own mini-pizza party. Experiment with elaborate and time-consuming dishes only at the most intimate of sit-down dinners. It's also a good idea to try the recipes before the party. They don't always turn out the way you expected.

If you think you'll need some help in the kitchen, consider hiring a high school or college student to help you with preparation, serving, and cleanup. Be sure you write down explicit instructions for your amateur servers so you can minimize your problems with burned food and ensure pleasant unobtrusive service. Or hire a caterer if you like, although it's more expensive and not quite as personal.

3

If you're preparing your own food, try to do as much of it in advance as possible. Have your food elegantly prepared, ready to serve, and easy to eat. If your party has a special theme, you may want to keep the food appropriate to it.

The question most hostesses worry about is "Will there be enough food?" I always recommend that you make more than you think you'll need, because you usually do need it. And you can always freeze the leftovers and save yourself from cooking for a few days after the party.

5. *Plan the serving of the food.*

Be sure you have enough trays and serving pieces to serve your food. You can borrow pieces from neighbors and friends, or rent the equipment from party stores and rental outlets.

Make your party especially nice by serving the food in unusual and appropriate ways. You might want to use some of the following: wicker baskets, wire baskets, cloth bags, scarves, decorative boxes, heart tins, old-fashioned tins, antique servers, unusual bowls, large copper pots, ceramic mugs, fancy glasses, rented champagne glasses, unusual jars, and large shells. You might even scoop out such fruits as watermelon, cantaloupe, oranges, or pumpkins and place the food inside the shells. Or try pita pockets, tortillas, or cream puff shells to hold the food.

Make sure you have enough tables on which to lay out the food. You might also use carts, counters, coffee tables, stools, unusual pieces of furniture, cutting boards, covered TV trays, or bookcases.

Cover your tables with decorative tablecloths or make your own by buying inexpensive lengths of bright and colorful fabric. Make your own napkin rings by cutting strips of ribbon and forming them into circles, or by covering paper tubes. Turn paper fans, contrasting colors of fabric, maps, large photos, fancy diapers, small straw mats, or inexpensive art reproductions into original and appropriate place mats.

6. *Plan the games and activities.*

Most parties benefit from a few carefully selected games and activities. They're often what makes a party stand out as special among a string of dull get-togethers. Pick out the games best suited to your theme and make sure they're appropriate for your particular group. But avoid the tired old games that are played at every party. If there will be winners, you need some prizes that relate to your theme. Try to pick out gifts that would be appropriate for both men and women, if both are attending your party, such as a bottle of champagne, a funny book, tickets to the theater, a coffee mug, a joke gift, a box of candy, a jar of gourmet sauce or seasonings, a puzzle, or a game. You might consider entertainment as an alternative to games, and hire a musician, magician, comedian, graphologist, fortune-teller, disc jockey, or juggler.

7. *Plan the decorations and atmosphere.*

Turning your party room into a seaside lagoon, a romantic fantasyland, or an intimate drawing room takes only a little imagination, a few props, and some construction paper. Think about your theme and create an atmosphere that fits your party. You might add a few chopsticks for your Chinese dinner, a checked tablecloth for your Italian spaghetti feed, hire a violinist for a little romance, or hang some black balloons for an "Over-the-Hill" party. Individual candles or flowers are a nice touch. Make place cards from paper fans, valentines, baggage claim tickets, and so on. And don't forget an appropriate centerpiece to set the stage—maybe a baby doll for the baby shower, a body outline for the murder party, some 78s for the fifties party, an edible appetizer tree, tagboard cutouts of Academy Awards, or just baskets full of related goodies and flowers.

The lighting at your party can also affect the mood. You might try dimmer switches, candles, colored light bulbs, lanterns, colored paper lamp covers, or flashing disco lights.

And fill the room with appropriate music. You may want classical for your dinner party, rock for your dance party, easy-listening for a romantic mood, country music for the Country Music Awards, or *Phantom of the Opera* for a Halloween bash. Your local record store has some long-playing tapes you may want to purchase, which will free you to enjoy the party rather than constantly attending to the music.

8. *Plan your invitations.*

Create your own invitations to suit your theme and to let your guests know what kind of party you'll be having. You might want to send out your party details on a balloon, a fan, a ticket, a postcard, a napkin, a travel brochure, a cookie, a small diaper, an artificial flower, a packet of seeds, a bubblegum card, a page from a book, a key, a paper hat, a wine label, an award certificate, a puzzle, a piece of cloth, a magazine ad, or a mask—whatever suits your theme. You could add some confetti to the envelope so it sprinkles out when the invitation is opened.

Be sure you go over your guest list to see that you haven't forgotten anyone. And don't forget to include an RSVP. Include on your invitation the following information: the date (and the day), the time (starting and ending), the place (will they need directions or a map), the occasion (fortieth birthday, baby shower), the details about the party ("It's a surprise!" "Bring your swimsuit!" "The shower has a kitchen theme"), and the attire (black tie optional, casual, grubs, swimwear only, your sexiest lingerie). If your party is very formal, send your invitations out three to four weeks before the event. If it's more casual, two weeks is about right.

9. *Plan your countdown.*

The best way to plan the countdown is to make a list of all the things you need to do, including guest list, food, supplies, chores, and other details. Here is a checklist to help you with your party plans:

Three weeks before the party:

Select reason for party, theme, and how you'll stage your party. Draw up guest list and send invitations. Decide on decorations and begin collecting and creating. Make food choices and prepare shopping list.

Few days before party:

Call any guests who have not responded. Clean house. Set up party room. Buy groceries and beverages. Make any food that can be made ahead and freeze it.

Day of party:

Decorate party room. Prepare rest of food. Check over party details and mentally run through the party again. Take a relaxing bath. Be ready for first guests.

10. *Plan for yourself.*

If you've exhausted yourself preparing for the party, you won't be able to enjoy it. And you've spent too much time and money to let that happen. If you have carefully planned and prepared for the party, you can spend that last day doing the fun things—setting up, getting yourself ready, and imagining the good time your guests will have.

WEDDING SHOWER

In the past, the wedding shower was given only by friends of the bride—never relatives. But the tradition has gradually changed and today anyone may honor the bride-to-be with a shower.

Romance is a perfect theme for your Wedding Shower. And there are many ways you can add your own special touches to create a romantic atmosphere.

First, decide whether you want to make it a "couples" shower or a "women only" shower. Many showers today include men so you might ask the bride-to-be if she'd like to have the groom and his friends invited, too.

Consider selecting a specific theme for the gift-buying, such as "kitchen gadgets," "romantic gifts," or "sexy nightwear." Or you might like the "Basket Surprise" shower, where each guest is assigned a different theme. For example, if you assign one or more guests to the "kitchen basket," they must bring a decorative basket, perhaps lined with a dish towel, and filled with such items as a baster, an egg timer, measuring cups, a strawberry stem-plucker—whatever—as long as it relates to the kitchen and fits into the basket. Other baskets might include the "bath basket" (soaps, washcloths, bath oils, etc.), "garden basket" (flower seeds, gloves, trowel, etc.), "bedroom basket" (sexy undies, nightwear, cologne, gorilla masks, etc.), "sewing basket" (pincushion, needle and thread, patches, ribbons, etc.), "ro-

8

mance basket" (dinner-for-two coupon, love coupons, sex manual, colored condoms, etc.), "picnic-for-two basket" (place setting for two, small bottle of champagne, wax-wrapped cheese, gourmet crackers, a book of poetry, etc.), "entertainment basket" (an X-rated video, a board game, tickets to the theater or movies, a coupon for an amusement park, etc.). And suggest they be creative with the baskets, too—how about a wicker basket, a flower basket, a clothes basket, or a wastebasket?

Another idea for a theme is a "Time of Day" shower. When you invite your guests, assign them a time of day and ask them to bring a gift appropriate for that time. For example, if you assign 8:00 A.M., the guest might bring an alarm clock, a pair of matching toothbrushes, a cozy bathrobe, some gourmet coffee. If the time is 2:00 P.M., your guest might bring a bottle of wine, two crystal glasses, and some massage oil for an "afternoon delight." This is a fun and creative party and works well for the bride who has already had a general household shower.

One of my friends attended a "Mad-Hatter's" shower, where each guest had created an unusual hat—covered with shower gifts attached by string or wire. Naturally there was an award for best hat.

Next you'll need to decide on the kind of shower you want to have. A luncheon or a dessert are popular for showers, but any format would work. You might even hold the shower in a fancy hotel restaurant and ask your guests to dress to the nines—hats, gloves, etc. Award a prize for the snootiest outfit, such as a toothbrush spray-painted gold.

And see if there might be a friend of the bride who's willing to co-host the shower with you. That way you'll have half the work and double the ideas.

INVITATIONS

Here are a few ideas for romantic invitations to your wedding shower. Be sure to include all the party information (date, time, place, guest of honor, kind of shower, hostess) and any special details (see page 6). And when selecting your party colors, borrow from the bride's wedding colors.

• Photocopy or reprint photographs of the bride and groom and cut the pictures into heart shapes. Glue them onto small white paper doilies and outline the heart photos with small pieces of colored cord. Write party details around outside of doily and mail in envelope.

• Photocopy the wedding invitation and use for front of invitation. Fold and write party details inside.

• Buy inexpensive toy wedding rings from the party supply store and tie two together with white ribbon. Write party details on small white card and tie to ribbon. Mail.

• Buy a small amount of colored netting and cut into 4-inch squares. Cut plastic wrap into same size and place on netting. Drop a tablespoon of colored rice in center and tie into small packet with colored ribbon. Place in envelope with card containing party details and mail. (To color rice, mix with a small amount of food coloring and water just until colored; drain, then dry on paper towels.)

• Write party details on white heart-shaped card and place in envelope. Fill envelope with a tablespoon of colored rice.

• Buy small bells at party supply store and tie two together with thin ribbon. Place "wedding bells" in small box with white tagboard cut into dove shape and fill with party information. Mail in padded envelope.

• Cut out heart from red construction paper and write invitation details on heart. Attach a narrow white lace border (paper or fabric) around heart and mail in envelope.

• Cut out heart shapes from 5-inch squares of red satin fabric and sew two hearts together, with right sides together, leaving one side open. Turn heart right side out. Stuff with sachet or batting, stitch closed, and write party information on red satin. Mail in padded envelope.

• Reproduce picture of bride and groom and glue onto tagboard. Cut into heart shape and write party information on back. Cut into puzzle pieces and drop into envelope.

• Buy miniature bride-and-groom cake toppers and attach to shower invitation.

DECORATIONS

The most beautiful wedding shower I have attended greeted me as I drove up to the home of the hostess. She had tied more than fifty helium and regular balloons to the front of her house—from trees, gutters, light posts, door-knobs, everywhere. From the end of each balloon dangled several lengths of white curling ribbon. The display was stunning!

Here are some more ideas for creating that romantic atmosphere:

• Fill a wall with balloons. To do this, tape strands of yarn from ceiling to floor along one wall of the party room, each strand about a foot from the next. To each yarn strand tie a balloon, alternating the bride's colors.

• Create a "wedding canopy" at the entryway by attaching crepe paper strands in the center of the entry ceiling and swagging them out toward either end of the room.

• Set bud vases with the bride's chosen flowers around the room for a sweet, romantic touch. Or attach single flowers from the bride's bouquet in wide bows and tie them around the room. If money is no object, fill the room with large bouquets of flowers in the bride's colors. You might even be able to rent plants and flowers for a garden party look.

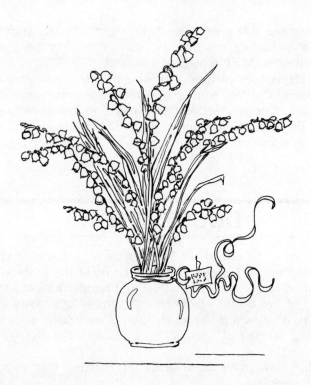

● Fill decorative clear glass jars, bowls, and vases with colored rice.

● Make a "towel cake" using the bride's colors by folding a washcloth, hand towel, and bath towel (new, of course, to be given as a gift at the end of the party) lengthwise into thirds, rolling them up like a jelly roll, and securing the ends with small safety pins. Set the rolled bath-towel layer on a large doily, the hand-towel layer in the center of the bath towel, and the washcloth layer on top of the hand towel. Swag around the "cake" with velveteen ribbon to make "icing" and secure with pins. Top with bride-and-groom figures from a cake store, or with a fresh flower corsage.

● If you've chosen a basket theme, set the filled baskets around the room. Attach ribbons to the handles.

- Collect pictures of the bride and groom from birth to present and mount the pictures on the wall with tape.
- Have a blowup made of the bride and groom's engagement picture and hang on wall. Give as gift after the party.
- Have blowups made of the bride and groom's baby pictures and hang on the wall side by side. Give as gift after the party.
- Rent a Bogey/Bacall video and have it running silently on the TV screen.
- Put up posters of famous romantic couples—Bogey/Bacall, Gable/Lombard, June/Ward Cleaver, Madonna/Sean Penn.
- Hang a wreath on the door with something old (an antique container), something new (a stylish bracelet), something borrowed (a library book on marriage), and something blue (a blue nightie).
- Substitute wreaths for baskets and have guests tie items to decorative wreaths, one for each season. Hang wreaths around room.
- Make corsages out of small household items, such as a new kitchen sponge, wire whisk, potato peeler, all tied with ribbons and a flower, for all the guests to wear during the party. When the party is over, ask them to hand over their corsages to the bride. (Or just make one corsage for the bride only.)
- Have romantic love songs playing in the background.
- Cut out red paper hearts and hang them from the ceiling with white yarn, or hang white paper doves from the ceiling.
- Have white candles burning throughout the room.

GAMES/ACTIVITIES

Games are popular at showers, and in keeping with our romantic theme, here are a few for the young at heart.

The Wedding Night

While the bride opens her shower gifts, discreetly record her exclamations, shrieks of joy, and oohs and ahhhs. As you take notes, write down *only* the comments that could be interpreted as a reaction to the "wedding night." After she has opened all her gifts, make the following announcement:

"There's an ancient marriage prophesy that states whatever the bride-to-be says during the gift-opening ceremony at her shower will be the very same words she speaks during her wedding night. If any of you happens to be passing by the newlywed's bedroom door on that sacred night, here are a few of the comments you might hear." Now read back all the comments you wrote down. You should get some wonderfully embarrassing statements like those I gathered at my sister's wedding shower—and when read in the context of the "wedding night," sound hilarious: "Ooh, it's just what I've always wanted! . . . I've never had one of these before! . . . If anybody ever wants to borrow this . . . Egads—it's enormous!"

The Newlywed Game

This will take a little pre-party preparation. If the party is women only, call the groom-to-be and ask him some questions about himself. For example: "What's your favorite dessert?" "Where did you go on your first date with the bride-to-be?" "What's your worst habit?" "What time do you go to bed?" "What does the bride-to-be cook the best?" "What was the last fight about?" "When did you get jealous last?" "What do you cook the best?" "What do you like to sleep in?" and so on. Ask him not to tell his fiancée about the game. Write each question on the front side of a $5'' \times 8''$ card and the answer on the back (or better yet, have the groom make a special appearance for this game and answer the questions himself). Pass out one question to each guest and have them take turns reading the questions aloud *without* letting the bride-to-be answer yet. Let each guest estimate how many right answers the bride will get—remember, she has not been told ahead of time about the game. (Be sure there are plenty of questions to go around at least once, maybe twice.) When the guests have guessed, have them read again, this time asking the bride to give her answers. Count up her number of correct answers and award a prize to the one who guesses closest.

This game works well with couples, too. Just follow the format of the television show, "The Newlywed Game."

Married Names

Pass out paper and pencil and ask guests to write down the names of some famous people who, when married, would form an interesting married name. For example, "If Phyllis Diller married Dobie Gillis, she'd be Phyllis Gillis." Or, "If Joan Collins married Tom Mix, she'd be Joan Collins-Mix." Or, "If Virginia Woolf married Thomas Mann, she'd be Virginia Woolf-Mann." The funniest one wins.

Rice Race

Fill 10 balloons with colored rice, then blow up balloons, very full, and tie off. Divide guests and line them up in two teams. Give the guests two forks each. On the count of three, pass a balloon to the first person on either side at the same time. They are to take the balloon with the forks and pass it to the next person, who is to do the same. The team with the balloon that makes it all the way down the line first, wins. If a balloon is popped along the way, a new balloon is begun again at the start. (As the guest of honor leaves the party, pop the rest of the rice-filled balloons over her head—outside.)

Pin the Chippendale

This game is for women only and is also perfect for the Bachelorette Party. Buy a large poster of your favorite Chippendale dancer, or other good-looking hunk. Cut out one G-string for each guest, plus an extra, from the black paper. Glue the extra one over the "bikini area" of the model and hang the picture on the wall. At game time, stick a thumbtack into one of the black G-strings, blindfold a guest, and have her try to pin the G-string in the appropriate place on the model. Give the winner the poster.

Beauty Aids

Cut out beauty ads from magazines, such as *Glamour, Vogue,* or *Seventeen,* omitting the product names. Mount the pictures onto construction paper. To play, hold up the ads or pass them around and have guests write the names of the products advertised on paper. Give the winner a beauty product.

Give-a-Hint

On the party invitation, ask each guest to bring a "helpful hint" that goes along with the gift. It can be a household hint or a marital hint, as long as it relates to the shower present.

As each gift is opened, ask the guest who brought it to read her helpful hint. Be sure they leave the hints with the gifts after all have been opened.

True Confessions

This will work if you have couples or just the women. Have each guest take a turn to answer the question "How did you meet your husband (or boyfriend)?" If you like, take it step further and ask "What has been your most embarrassing moment during your relationship?" If you've got an especially close group, how about a round of "The first time" with-your-partner stories. Award prizes to the most interesting stories.

How to Have a Perfect Marriage

Divide a sheet of paper in half by making a line in the center. Repeat for each guest. Write a typical marital problem on the top half of each sheet, such as "If your husband wants to watch football all weekend . . ." "If your husband flirts with another woman . . ." "If you burn the toast . . ." "If his mother is driving you crazy . . ." Use the "If . . ." format.

Pass out the papers to each guest and ask them to write a piece of advice for the problem on the *bottom* half, completing the sentence. For example, if a guest reads "If you burn the toast . . ." she might answer with ". . . get another piece."

After everyone has put down her answer, tear off the top half of the paper and mix up the problems, then mix up the answers and pass them out to the guests. Ask the bride to pick a problem and read it aloud, and have the *first* person on her left read her answer, followed by the next person for the next question, and so on. You should get some funny pieces of scrambled advice, such as "If you burn the toast, unplug the TV set."

Here Comes the Bride

If you have a small group, use the bride-to-be for this game. If you have a large group, divide into teams and choose a "bride" from each group.

17

Hand the group several rolls of toilet paper and have them "dress" the bride. If you have teams, award prizes for most creative, funniest, sexiest, and so on.

REFRESHMENTS

After you've chosen the type of shower you want to have, you'll be able to plan the refreshments. If you're planning only drinks and appetizers, you might want to start off with a glass of champagne garnished with a strawberry or two maraschino cherries, or serve smooth and slushy strawberry daiquiris. Here's a special one—mix ½ pint strawberry ice cream with 2 ounces rum in the blender and whirl until smooth. Frosty and delicious!

Baked Brie topped with sliced strawberries and green apple slices makes a beautiful and delicious appetizer. Bake the Brie inside a round loaf of French bread for 10 minutes at 350°F for a hearty treat.

Melon balls wrapped in prosciutto and secured with fancy toothpicks look inviting in a scooped out cantaloupe shell, or fill an ornately carved watermelon shell with a variety of fruits.

If you are hosting a luncheon, make mini-croissant sandwiches filled with deviled ham or turkey.

For dessert, serve ladyfingers topped with your favorite frosting and trimmed with walnuts. These are simple and elegant. Or dip strawberries in semisweet and white chocolate and arrange on a large platter. Or how about individual servings of chocolate mousse, with white chocolate curls sprinkled on top?

A dessert as simple as French vanilla ice cream in sherbet or champagne glasses and topped with white sugar doves is an elegant addition to your party.

If you're serving a cake at your shower, decorate it (or ask the bakery to do it) with sugar doves, toy gold rings, or flowers in the bride's colors. You might want it to be a small version of a wedding cake, or have the bakery make it in the shape of a book, to resemble the wedding album.

And if you're serving a cake for dessert, you might want to add some sherbet on the side, selecting flavors that match the bride's colors.

PRIZES/GIFTS/FAVORS

You'll need some romance-related prizes for the game winners and some favors for the rest of the guests.

Prizes

• Give the winner a coffee mug covered with hearts and mushy message.
• A box of candy is a traditionally romantic gift—and loved by all.
• A bottle of champagne.
• A romance novel.
• A heartthrob record by Julio Inglesias or other torch singer.
• Two champagne glasses.
• Tickets to a romantic comedy.
• Massage oil.
• Sexy underwear.

Gift Suggestions for the Bride:

• A box of stationery with her new name embossed at the top.
• Return address labels with the new name.
• A brass nameplate for the front door inscribed with the new Mr. and Mrs. name.
• A photo album for all the wedding or shower pictures.
• A book on love, marriage, or sex.
• A plant for the new home.

- A pair of white silk stockings or white silk panties for the wedding.
- A sexy nightie.
- The wedding invitation in an elegant frame.
- Something from the "Basket" theme list.

Favors

- Wrap some Jordan almonds in netting and tie with a white ribbon.
- Send each guest home with a small white candle to bring to the wedding and light during the kiss.
- Buy several romance magazines, roll them up, and tie with ribbon.
- Fill small heart-shaped boxes with Red Hots.
- Give each woman a silk red rose or flower arrangement used for the party.

BABY SHOWER

Today anyone may host a baby shower—relative or friend. The first decision you'll need to make is when to have the shower—before or after the baby is born. Some prospective parents prefer to wait until after the birth, others like the more traditional shower before the baby comes. Unless it's a surprise, it's a good idea to ask the prospective parents which they prefer. Also, some pregnant women are uncomfortable in the last few weeks before the baby is born and may not feel up to attending the event. Or there may be a particular time of day when mom-to-be feels at her best, so be sure to check with her.

Next you'll want to decide whether it will be all women or whether it will include men. More and more men are becoming involved with every aspect of parenthood, including the shower.

Baby showers often have themes. You can offer the parents-to-be a shower exclusively devoted to baby clothes (diapers, T-shirts, rompers, snowsuits), baby toys (rattles, music boxes, stacking towers, pull toys), bath items (tub, puppet washcloths, baby toiletries, bathinette), or you can assign each guest a "time" and ask that gifts be made appropriate to the selected time, as in the Wedding Shower. If the time is "noon," your guest might bring mealtime items (dish, silver spoon, bottles, heating bowls). Bedtime gear (sleepers, sleeping bags, musical teddy bears, cradle) would be perfect for 7:00 P.M. You might have a shower devoted to outfitting the nursery instead of the baby (posters, mobiles, furniture, bedding). Or, for a change, make it a shower for the new parents, with books on kids, tickets for a night out, help with housecleaning.

If dad is invited, you might tell each guest to bring along a gag gift especially for him—ear plugs for sleeping through the night, *TV Guide* for the late-night feedings, a copy of *David, We're Pregnant!* or *Hi Mom! Hi Dad!*, both by Lynn Johnston ($3.50, Meadowbrook, Deephaven, MN: 1977), a copy of *How to Be a Pregnant Father,* by Peter Mayle ($12.00, Lyle Stuart, Secaucus, NJ: 1977), a copy of *Babies and Other Hazards of Sex,* by Dave Barry ($4.95, Rodale Press, Emmaus, PA: 1984), or a rubber lap protector.

Another idea you might want to incorporate is the offering of a special gift for mother-to-be as well as baby. This would be a good time to fill her maternity suitcase with a new nightie, a baby-care book, travel shampoo, a new maternity gown, a breast-feeding blouse. We sometimes overlook the guest of honor in favor of the new arrival and this is a nice way to make her feel special.

Or give your party an overall theme, such as Teddy Bears, Sugar and Spice, or The Cabbage Patch, with invitations, decorations, and so on to set the atmosphere.

Finally, decide what kind of party you'd like to have. A brunch, a luncheon, a dessert, or perhaps an afternoon tea would work well for a baby shower. Just be sure to check with the parents so they'll be at their best for this special occasion.

INVITATIONS

Begin your party plans with an appropriate invitation. Ask the guests to bring along a baby picture of themselves for a game. Here are some suggestions for your baby shower:

• You can create little "diaper" invitations by cutting out triangles from pink and blue construction paper or felt. Write your party details on one side of the triangle with a fine-tip felt pen, then fold the triangle like a diaper and secure it with a cute diaper pin from the baby store.

• Cut out pictures of babies from magazines and glue them into a piece of white tagboard with a cartoon bubble that contains the party information.

• Send your guests a yellow (or pink or blue) bubble gum cigar with a tag attached announcing "It's a Baby Shower" and the details.

• Borrow baby pictures of the parents-to-be and photocopy them. Arrange them together on a pink or blue tagboard card and write the party details on the reverse side.

• Fold a sheet of green construction paper in half and draw a picture of a cabbage. Cut out the cabbage with the fold at the bottom so you can open up the cabbage. Glue a baby picture inside and write your party information inside.

• Pick up some little plastic babies, or other baby decorations, at the cake and party supply store and tie your invitation card to one of the items with pink or blue ribbon. Stick everything in an envelope and mail.

• Cut out pink or blue pacifiers from tagboard and write party details on one side. Tie with ribbon.

• Check the variety store for baby paper dolls. Cut out dolls and outfits and write your party information on one of the outfits, then mail to guests.

• Make up tiny birth certificates using quality paper and careful handwriting. Fill in party details instead of baby details.

• Cut out or create pictures of teddy bears to use as invitations.

- Cut out small hand or foot prints and write invitation on one side.
- Create your own rhyme, borrowing from an old nursery rhyme or other favorite. Change the words to fit your party. For example, "Roses are red, violets are blue, we're having a shower, and hope you'll come, too." Decorate invitation with cutouts from an inexpensive nursery rhyme book.
- Make a hospital bracelet like the one they attach to baby after the birth. Cut white tagboard into strips and write party information on both sides. Cover with clear Contact paper and secure into circle by punching a small hole on both ends and tying together. Mail to guests.
- Rip a page from an old baby name book and write your party information around the edges.
- Send a picture of the very pregnant mom glued to a card with party information on the back.
- Cut out three squares from construction paper in pink, blue, and yellow. Write, A, B, and C in each one and write party information on the backs. Drop into envelope and mail to guests.

DECORATIONS

With a little imagination and a few props, you can turn your party room into a make-believe nursery. Try some of the following suggestions to set the mood for your shower:

- Cover the table with a pink or blue paper tablecloth and set the opposite color plates around. Or cover the table with a baby blanket and a plastic cover on top to protect it.
- Make name tags for the guests from pink and blue triangles cut from felt and folded into diapers. Make place mats from diapers dyed pink and blue. Or cut out construction paper place mats and glue on pictures of babies cut from magazines.

- Write names of guests on outside of small felt diapers and pin onto guests as they arrive.
- Ask each guest to bring a baby photo. Collect and mount them on a sheet of yellow construction paper as the guests come in the door. Tape them carefully to a wall in the party room, being sure none of their names show, so you can play a game with them later on.
- If you can find a "Super Baby" pajama outfit or "Super Hero" underwear (available at many department and discount stores in the infant/toddler section), dress up a baby doll or Cabbage Patch Kid in the outfit and set it in an infant seat (or other piece of baby equipment) in the center of table or room.
- Hang cute diaper pins from the ceiling using pink, yellow, and blue ribbon. Or hang miscellaneous baby items instead. Cut out little storks and hang them from the ceiling.
- Place baskets of baby items in the center of the table for a centerpiece. Or arrange a collection of baby toys for a centerpiece. Or a stack of small colorful blocks makes a nice, simple centerpiece.
- Borrow some dolls and doll furniture and set up a little display for atmosphere.
- Play nursery music in the background.
- Tie pink and blue balloons to the backs of the chairs.
- Place green cutout cabbages around the walls with little baby pictures peeping over the edges.

● Double up a pair of pastel baby socks and pin them together for a corsage for the guest of honor.

● Serve party drinks in clear plastic baby bottles (or glass ones if you find them). Tie with pink and blue ribbon, and insert pink and blue straws.

● Cut out tiny baby clothes from pink, blue, and yellow felt and pin to a small clothesline. Hang on the wall or secure to stands and set on table as centerpiece.

● Buy inexpensive bibs, or make them from terrycloth or plastic fabric, and use them as place mats for the party.

GAMES/ACTIVITIES

Baby showers are a great time to play a few funny games. Here are some we've had the most fun with:

The Baby Food Taste

This is a terrific game that provides a lot of funny expressions on the faces of the guests. Buy eight jars of baby food (get a variety—cereal, fruit, veggies, meat, mixtures) and remove or cover the labels with foil so they cannot be read. Write a number on the side of the jar with a felt-tip pen and keep track of the flavors by number on a separate sheet of paper. Pass out paper plates, plastic spoons, and paper and pencil to all the guests. Ask the guests to make eight circles on the plate and label each with a number, *outside* the circle. Place a plastic spoon in each of the baby food jars. Begin the game by announcing that since their babies have to eat this stuff, it's only fair that you moms and dads taste it first. (Watch the reaction!) Then pass around jar #1, ask everyone to spoon out a small amount onto the first circle on their plates, then taste it with their individual spoons. Have them write their answers on the sheet of paper—and tell them to keep the answers to themselves— no cheating! When all eight jars have been passed around, announce the real flavors and have everyone count their correct answers. I'll bet no one gets them all. . . .

Guess the Baby Gadget

Collect 10 baby items, e.g, nose syringe, thermometer, medicine giver, nipple, pacifier, comb, diaper, baby book, rubber pants, bottle brush.

Buy 20 paper bags, preferably 10 in pink and 10 in blue, for double-bag thickness. Place one bag inside another to increase the thickness of bag (helps prevent tearing) and put one of the ten baby items in each bag. Number the bags from 1 to 10 on the outside and staple each bag closed. Explain to the guests that they are to feel the *outside* of the bag and write down exactly what the baby item inside is. Pass the bags around and let everyone feel each bag for about thirty seconds, then pass them on. When all have had a chance to feel the bags and write their answers, open the bags and pull out the baby items. Present the baby items to the parents-to-be and a prize to the winner.

The Baby Business

Tear out eight to ten pictures of baby products from baby magazines, such as *American Baby, Parents, Working Mother,* and so on, and cut off the *names* of the products. For example, you might rip out a photo of a little kid who's crying because his teeth hurt, but cut off the word "Numzit." Glue the photos onto pink and blue construction paper or tagboard. Ask guests to write down the product name as you hold up each card for all to see. The one with the most correct answers is the winner.

Guess Who?

Now it's time to figure out who all those funny-looking kids are. Hang baby pictures of guests on the wall. Give your guests a chance to look closely at the photos and guess who's who.

Big Belly Estimate

Give each guest a 5-foot piece of yarn and ask them to mark off with a knot what they think the circumference of the expectant mother's tummy is. Then measure the pieces around her waist to see who's right. Or just ask your guests how many baby safety pins it would take to go around the pregnant belly. Then connect enough safety pins to fit around mother and determine winner.

Take My Advice

As the mother-to-be opens each shower gift, ask each guest to give her one piece of advice that was very helpful in the first few months of parenthood. You might want to share some of the worst advice, as well.

Another version of this activity is to pass around a nice bound blank book and have each guest write "Something I learned too late" that relates to raising babies. After all have had a chance to write their memories, have the guest of honor read them all aloud. (You can play a version of this game at the Wedding Shower also.)

New Parenthood Poetry

Ask each guest to bring a poem, an excerpt from a story, or some other famous passage that expresses some aspect of new parenthood. Have each guest read the selection to the mother-to-be as she opens each gift.

Crib Notes

On small slips of paper, write down an old-wives' tale, a line of poetry, a quote from a baby book, or some other statement about baby-raising. Place the papers in a basket and pass it around. Ask each guest to draw a slip of paper, read the quote, and make a comment about it. Don't let guests read their quotes ahead of time—this should be off the tops of their heads.

My Most Embarrassing Moment

Ask each guest to share a most embarrassing moment as a new parent. This game helps everyone tame the "Super Mom" myth and proves to be a lot of fun.

Child Development

On each slip of paper, write a typical childhood event. You might have baby's first tooth, baby's first step, baby's first word, baby's first haircut, junior's first day of kindergarten, junior's first trip to the dentist, junior's first bike, junior's first girlfriend, junior's first day at camp, junior's first car, junior's graduation.

Number each slip in order of development and give each slip to a guest. Call off by number and have that guest act out the parent's reaction to baby's latest development. Have the rest of the party members guess the stage.

REFRESHMENTS

Along with a fancy cake, you might want to serve one of the refreshments suggested in the Wedding Shower chapter, or create something new.

If you're having a luncheon, ask the bakery to tint some loaves of bread pink and blue to use for sandwiches. Make the sandwiches with salmon and cream cheese, or cream cheese (tinted, if you like) mixed with walnuts and raisins, or any other filling of your choice.

For dessert, serve hollowed-out oranges filled with orange sherbet and topped with whipped cream, or make meringue shells tinted pink and blue and fill with strawberries and blueberries. Top with a dollop of whipped cream, also tinted pink or blue.

Pregnant women are not encouraged to drink alcohol during pregnancy, so serve a nonalcoholic punch made from

clear, noncaffeinated soft drink and cranberry juice or club soda and fruit juice. Float large spoonfuls of raspberry sherbet in your punch bowl and add a spoonful to each glass as you serve it.

Your baker can probably create an unusual cake, in the shape of a rattle, diaper, or baby bottle, or decorate the top with your favorite baby cartoon. Or go with the traditional petit fours, ladyfingers, or puff pastries that always delight any crowd.

PRIZES/GIFTS/FAVORS

You'll need some prizes for the winners of all those games, so wrap a few of the following:

- A copy of Dave Barry's *Babies and Other Hazards of Sex* ($4.95, Rodale Press, Emmaus, PA: 1984).
- Gag gifts, such as packages of contraceptives or a home pregnancy test.
- Something romantic that can be shared with a partner—a block of cheese, a loaf of French bread, or a bottle of wine.
- Gifts that contain the word "baby." For example, a "Baby Ruth" candy bar, "Sugar Babies," "Babe" cologne, a book about Babe Ruth, a "Baby Doll" nightie, and so on.
- A book on where babies come from.

- A clear baby bottle full of candy, mints, nuts, or jelly beans.

If your guests need ideas for gifts, you might suggest one of the following:

- All contribute to one large gift, such as a baby swing, and then each guest also bring along one small gift.
- A list of all the parks, baby classes, pediatricians, discount baby clothes stores, and so on, from your community.
- Have each guest bring a name suggestion for a boy and a girl on a cute card, along with a little history about the name and some famous people with the same name. If the name happens to be selected by the parents, send the guest a small prize.
- Ask each guest to bring a box of disposable diapers along with a gift, wrapped in fancy paper and ribbons. Or ask them to wrap the diaper box in pink, blue, or yellow paper. Cut out large alphabet letters from construction paper and glue them to the sides of the boxes after they have arrived and set them up in the party room to look like a gigantic stack of baby blocks.
- Books on baby care, books on what to name the baby, or baby books.
- Coupons worth hours of baby-sitting, housecleaning, or helping out with laundry. Or have each guest sign up for one night of bringing dinner to the new family.
- A quilt square in a particular theme (alphabet, toys, colors) and someone to sew them all together before the party. Then present it to the new parents as a wonderful finale.
- Coupon good for a portrait of the new baby and a silver frame. Or have each guest bring along a roll of film nicely wrapped, in addition to her present.
- A savings account or savings bond for baby.
- A tiny T-shirt with the words "Class of '99" (or whatever year the baby will graduate from high school).
- A night on the town.

For favors, send the guests home with a small gift for their own children, such as a coloring book, crayons, a Golden Book, and so on. (If they don't have children, perhaps for a niece or nephew or neighbor's child.) Or get them each a small teddy bear pin or other cute accessory. A funny favor that's easy to make is a bottle of "birth control pills." Save your old medicine bottles or ask the pharmacist for some empties and fill them with small round candies. Make up labels that read "Birth Control Pills. To prevent pregnancy, place between legs," or some other silly instructions.

BIRTHDAY PARTY

You can host a birthday party any year, but the big milestones—thirty, forty, and fifty—are the most popular for big birthday bashes, especially the surprise variety. Birthday parties are a great boost for those who dread those milestones and a wonderful way to remind the guest of honor how celebrated he or she really is.

Think about the kind of party you want to have. Almost anything will work, but cocktail parties and dinner parties are the most popular. Or try something different, like an early-morning breakfast party, a surprise picnic, or a progressive dinner party with surprises at each home (see Moving Away, page 125).

You might design the party around the birthday person's vocation (have the guests dress up as "patients" for the doctor) or hobby (all arrive as a favorite detective for the armchair sleuth). Or focus the party on a popular theme today—the "Over-the-Hill" party, with parodies of growing older.

Check the last chapter in the book for themes for your birthday bash, or try one of these:

- A gourmet picnic at a local park.
- A fish fry where guests bring their own "catch" to grill on your barbecue.
- A skating or skiing party.
- A "Middle Ages" party with a Camelot theme.
- A party combined with the special guest's favorite activity—football game, horse race, bowling, and so on.
- Invite an entertainer—a comedian, fortune-teller, or singer.
- A road rally for car buffs or bicycling friends.
- Rent a local diner or other "dive" for a nostalgia party.
- Hold it at the high school gym and invite old friends to give cheers, play the school song, and so on.
- Rent a houseboat, sailboat, or other small boat for a floating party on the water.
- Have a sock hop with songs and props from the teen-age years.
- Host a "Big Birthday Party," with oversized decorations and large numbers of small gifts, such as a case of beer, a crate of bubble bath, a carton of sweets.
- Choose an ethnic theme, such as an Italian spaghetti feed or a Mexican fiesta or a Caribbean night.

SURPRISE!

Most people like to make birthday parties a surprise. If that's your plan, be sure to get an assistant to host the party until your arrival or to get the guest of honor out of the way. Here are some ideas for pulling it off:

• Take the guest of honor out to dinner and have an assistant welcome the invited guests. When you return from dinner—surprise!

• Ask the guest of honor to go get the baby-sitter across town. When he or she gets there, have the sitter's parent explain there's been a mix-up and the sitter has already been driven to the home. This gives you time to let your guests in and set up a simple party atmosphere. When he or she returns—surprise!

• Take the guest of honor out to dinner, but get halfway there and remember you forget your wallet. Have the guests waiting at a neighbor's house, ready to move into your home when you leave. When your return home, go in for the wallet while your spouse waits in the car. Call out that there's a phone call for him or her—surprise!

• Take the guest of honor out for a full evening and get a stomachache halfway through. Return home for—surprise!

• Invite friends to assemble at a restaurant. When you and the birthday person arrive—surprise!

• Plan a surprise lunch with a group of friends, all wearing "Barbara's 40th" T-shirts (the name of the birthday person).

• Send the guest of honor on an errand to the store, then a friend's house. Have the friend keep him or her busy for a while, then call when he leaves—surprise!

• Have the party at a friend's house.

• Have the party a few days before or a short time after the official birthday.

• Have an early-morning surprise party or one late at night, to catch the suspicious ones off guard.

- Plan a surprise party for a friend who has a real or imaginary birthday near the real guest of honor's, then turn the tables on him—he's helped out at his own surprise party!
- Have all the guests meet at a neighbor's, gather all the food and props, then walk en masse to the honoree's house and ring the bell—surprise!

INVITATIONS

Birthday invitations can be created from anything appropriate to your theme. Here are a few suggestions you might want to consider:

- If your party is to be a surprise, the best way to invite your guests is to call them—that way there's no evidence lying around for the honored guest to discover. And stress the importance of being prompt.
- Another distinct way of inviting guests to a birthday party is the balloon invitation. Blow up a balloon and write your party information on it with a felt-tip pen. If it's a surprise party, you might add something like "Shhh . . ." or "Don't Blow It!" Deflate the balloon and stick it in an envelope with instructions to blow it up.
- Make the balloon invitation and hand-deliver the inflated balloon in a large box.
- Photocopy a birth certificate or old birth announcement on parchment paper for the cover of the invitation, and add the party details instead of the birth details.
- Photocopy pictures of the birthday guest as a baby (or an adult), mount on colored tagboard, and write your party details underneath the photo.
- If your party has an "Over-the-Hill" theme, send a black balloon or black invitation, include black armbands, and suggest to your guests that they dress in mourning. If

you're designing your party around the vocation or hobby, send out something related, such as an appointment card for the doctor or a mysterious puzzle for the armchair detective.

• Draw a simple birthday cake on a colorful tagboard card and write your party information around it. Tape a small birthday candle on top of the cake, wrap card in tissue to protect it, and mail in envelope.

• Write your party invitation on a colorful square of tagboard and wrap the invitation with birthday party paper. Or take it a step further and drop the card into a small box and wrap in birthday paper. Mail to guests.

• Get a copy of the front page of a newspaper from the day and year your birthday guest was born and reproduce it once. Cut out one of the articles and substitute your own, beginning with a headline about the guest's birth and following with details about the party. (If you have a friend with a computer, you can make up a realistic column. Or get a printer to do it.) Reproduce your paste-up and mail to guests. Maybe ask guests to dress up in the style of the year he or she was born.

• Have an artist draw a caricature of the birthday person and use reproductions for your invitation.

• Write your party information on a party horn or party hat and place in envelope.

• Photocopy a calendar sheet on colored paper and mark the date of the party on the calender with details.

• Cut out the horoscope from a newspaper, magazine, or book and substitute a typewritten horoscope predicting the birthday party. Give details and mail.

• Attach a birthday sticker to the envelope, alerting your guests to the invitation inside. Put confetti inside the envelope.

• You might ask your guests to write a funny poem or anecdote and bring it along to use during one of the games on pages 40–41.

• Choose some aspect from your special theme, such as a picture of a fish if it's to be a fish fry, or a map for the road rally, and mail it to your guests with party information on the back.

DECORATIONS

Create a festive atmosphere for your birthday party with some of the following ideas:

● Fill the room with colorful streamers, confetti, and balloons. You might want to create a gazebo with streamers in the center of your party room by attaching different colors to the middle of the ceiling, draping them out toward the walls, and letting the ends hang down the sides of the wall. Or hang a large balloon or paper ball in the center of the room and drape paper curls over it. Sprinkle confetti on the tables and floor. Hang balloons from the ceiling.

● Fill a closet with balloons and have the guest of honor hang up a coat—watch the look of surprise when the balloons tumble out!

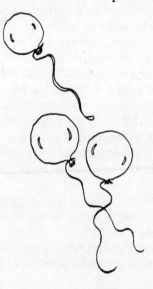

- Fill the birthday person's car with balloons as an extra surprise.
- Make a donation and have a few members of the high school band come and serenade the birthday person during the party.
- If you want to have a "This Is Your Life" theme, run a time-line along one wall chronicling the honoree's life from birth to present in pictures. Mount them on silver stars. Add funny captions to the photos. (See Games/Activities for more ideas on "This Is Your Life" theme.) Decorate the room with stars.
- Collect items from the baby book or the year of the birthday person's birth and turn them into a centerpiece.
- Line the walls with pictures of famous people born the same day as the birthday guest. You can find this information at the library in various almanacs, then get the pictures from movie magazines or poster stores.
- Find the day's horoscope in a newspaper, magazine, or book and copy it onto a large sheet of tagboard. Or make up your own funny one.
- Cut out silhouettes of party friends and put them on the walls, or do the same with "mystery guests" for the "This Is Your Life" party.
- Black should be the color scheme at your "Over-the-Hill" party. Cover the table in a black paper tablecloth and use black plates, napkins, and so on. (Many stationery stores carry a line of paper party products called "Over-the-Hill" that should delight the guests.) Place the gag gifts in the center of the table, with two black candles on either side. Blow up black balloons and hang them from the ceiling. Greet the guest with a wheelchair and dress the spouse in black.
- Pick out a line of paper products with a youthful theme—Mickey Mouse or Barbie plates and cups, or go right for the baby shower items that feature cute little babies.
- Fill the party room with helium balloons (they'll float to the ceiling) with colored ribbons dangling. You can rent a helium tank to fill the balloons if you're going to go all out.

• Play music from the honoree's teenage years and hang a blowup of his or her graduation picture.

GAMES/ACTIVITIES

Following your chosen theme, there are several different games and activities you can do to add a little fun to your party.

• If you're hosting a "This Is Your Life" birthday party, you'll need to do a little preparation. Contact some special old friends that your guest of honor hasn't seen in quite a while and invite them to be "mystery guests" at the party. Ask them to bring along a poem or funny anecdote about the birthday person. When they arrive, do silhouettes of their heads on black paper and tape them around the walls with white question marks inside. Then tape-record their poems or stories and hide the mystery guests in a back room. After the honoree arrives, begin the "This Is Your Life" activity. Holding a large book with pre-written notes inside, tease your birthday star with a few clues to the identity of the first mystery guest. Then play the tape recording. Allow time to guess, and then bring out the mystery guest.

• If you've created a time-line with photographs of the birthday person's life, assign a picture to each guest and have them write a funny comment. When all are finished, have the guests read their comments in order.

• Turn your birthday party into a "Roast." Provide a long banquet table to seat your guests, with a special spot in the middle for the "roastee." Rent, make, or borrow a podium and allow each guest to take a turn at the podium, to read a funny story, recall a nice memory, or tell an anecdote about the birthday person.

• Take each guest aside and video-tape a funny anecdote

or poem about the birthday person. Play the tape during the party and give as a gift afterward.

● Sometime before the party, make a video tape of still pictures chronicling milestones in the birthday guest's life. Add a funny story line to follow the pictures as their life unfolds, pausing several minutes on each photograph. Play the tape at the party.

● Have each guest bring a wrapped memento from some event they've shared with the birthday honoree. It might be a broken ski from a disastrous ski trip, a shirt with a wine stain from a wild party, or whatever. Have each guest explain the significance of the gift as it's opened.

● Hire an electronic message company or skywriter to write Happy Birthday to the birthday person in the sky.

● If your theme revolves around a vocation or hobby, play "Liar's Trivia." Do a little research on the theme subject, digging out unusual questions about the vocation or hobby. At party time, ask one of the questions and tell the birthday person to give a convincing response. Have the first guest to his or her left verify or deny the answer by saying "I agree" or "I disagree." Give gag gifts related to the theme to anyone who is right.

● Quiz a relative or good friend about embarrassing moments in the birthday person's life. Write each one on a piece of paper. At party time, have each guest pick a slip of paper and act out the situation. Have the birthday person guess what's happening.

● Dig out a few interesting facts about the birthday person—an unusual job, an odd middle name, a secret hobby—and write them on slips of paper. Then make up several strange facts that are *not* true about the person. At party time, mix up the true and false facts, pick one, and read it aloud. Ask the first person on the left to tell whether it's true or false. Give a gag gift for a correct answer.

● Rent a wheelchair and have the honoree spend the evening in it. Open the gag gifts for the "Over-the-Hill" party.

REFRESHMENTS

Most birthday parties feature a large, decorated sheet cake from the bakery—it's simple, makes a nice centerpiece, and feeds the crowd without a lot of hassle. You might want to have the baker make up something unusual to tie in with your theme—perhaps a cartoon that features a favorite hobby—or ask that two cakes be shaped in the birthday person's age, with a big 3 (4, 5) and 0.

But if you want to make your own stunning birthday cake with little effort, try this: Buy a chocolate cake mix or prepare one from scratch. Pour into a large sheet cake pan. Spoon on 1 can of cherry pie filling and swirl through batter. Bake as directed. Top cake with whipped cream and decorate with maraschino cherries.

Or buy or bake a large chocolate sheet cake and separate it into three layers after the cake has cooled, using a length of thread or dental floss. Cover first layer with whipped cream and sliced strawberries, then top with second layer and repeat. Top with third layer, cover with whipped cream, and decorate top with small whole strawberries. Drizzle fudge topping over the whole cake and serve.

Or, instead of the traditional birthday cake, make an ice cream cake. Make a sheet cake in birthday person's favorite flavor. Separate cake into two sheets when cool. Open rectangular half-gallon carton and slice ice cream ½ inch thick. Place between cake layers. Return to freezer while preparing frosting. Frost cake quickly and return to freezer until serving time. Top with strawberries, cherries, chocolate curls, flaky coconut, or chopped nuts and serve immediately.

Or make your own cake that's a little less sugary by preparing a sugar-free angel food cake or shortbread covered with berries and whipped cream. And don't forget the champagne—at least for the toast while serving the cake. Then you can switch to wine or a sparkling punch.

Also have munchies on hand for the guests. Flavored

popcorn is a great crowd pleaser and easy to prepare. Pop corn according to directions, drizzle with butter, and mix in one of the following: Parmesan cheese, lemon-herb seasoning, Mexican seasoning, dry sour cream seasoning and onion salt, powdered Cheddar cheese.

PRIZES/GIFTS/FAVORS

If the birthday party game requires a prize, award one of the following:

- T-shirt, bumper sticker, or pin that says, "Carolyn is 40" or "I'm a friend of Bill's." You can make these the party favors, too. It's kind of nice seeing a whole group of people wearing your name on their chests.
- Tickets to a play or movie with the birthday person as your escort.
- A book on parties or a party cookbook.
- A book about friendship.
- A coffee mug with a saying about friendship.
- A bottle of wine with the birthday person's personalized label.
- A friendship ring.
- A tin of cookies.
- Gourmet coffee, gourmet chocolate sauce, or other gourmet item.
- A poster of the birthday person.
- A plant.
- An apothecary jar filled with jelly beans.

For gift-giving ideas for the birthday person, you might suggest things that will remind the guest of honor of the wonderful friendships he or she has made over the years. How about:

• An item symbolizing a past experience together that will be appreciated and treasured by the guest of honor. For example, if you attended a Mozart concert together, pick up a copy of *Amadeus*. If you vacationed together in Hawaii, bring along a poster of Waikiki Beach. If you took a night class on Computer Literacy for a semester, buy a game for his or her Apple II. If he's your fishing buddy, get him a box of hand-tied flies or fishing lures.

• An address book with all the friends listed.

• A giant chocolate chip cookie. Make the recipe according to package directions, shape into heart on foil-covered cookie sheet, and bake 5 to 10 minutes longer than instructed. Remove carefully and slide onto cardboard cut to shape, write Happy Birthday greeting with icing, and wrap in plastic wrap.

• A box of fine cigars.

• Tickets to a sporting event, such as baseball, football, hockey.

• Some blank video tapes or a video-taped movie.

• A string of lottery tickets equal to the honoree's age. For example, if it's a fortieth birthday, give forty lottery tickets.

• A T-shirt for someone who's turning forty that says "Just turned 30." (Be sure it's ten years younger than the real birthday!)

• Some new piece of sporting equipment to keep the honoree in shape—a basketball, a tennis racket, and so on.

• A box full of gourmet foods the honoree would probably never buy—a jar of caviar, gourmet popcorn, decadent fudge sauce, fancy olive oil, fancy vinegar, etc.

• If your emphasis is on the "Big Birthday," ask your guests to go for quantity. A case of wine coolers, a bag full of bikini underwear, a box full of fancy soaps, a carton of candy bars.

• One interesting idea for your own gift to the birthday person is to have a star named after him or her. For around $35, the International Star Registry will name a star for your friend, and send him or her a framable registration

sheet, the location of the star, and a map of the con-
stellations. Then you can take your friend outside, point
toward the heavens and say, "Don't worry. I just made you
immortal." For more information, call 800-282-3333.

- If it's a birthday for a senior who will be eighty or older,
you can have the President send a special birthday card to
the birthday person if you write four weeks ahead to
"Greetings Office of the White House, Washington, D.C.
20500." Tell them the full name, address, and occasion.

If you're hosting an "Over 30" party, half the fun is the
gifts. The subject is ripe for jokes and everyone has a good
laugh, as the birthday person tears the wraps from his or her
new collection of anti-aging aids. If some of the guests need
ideas, you might suggest the following:

- Denture cleanser (for that new set of choppers you'll be
getting).
- A foggy mirror (so you can't see your wrinkles).
- A toothless comb (for the gentleman who's "losing it").
- A fan (for those hot flashes).
- A magnifying glass (for the poor eyesight).
- Birthday control pills (a little medicine bottle filled
with jelly beans with a homemade label that reads "Birth-
day Control Pills: Take one once a year to control birth-
days").
- A tube of Detane (for men only).
- Grecian formula (for those distinguished-looking gray
hairs).
- A cane.
- A fishing-tackle box (to carry all those medications in).
- Baby food (no teeth).
- A subscription to *Modern Maturity*.
- A copy of *The Joy of Sex*.
- A bottle of Geritol or iron tablets.
- Granny shoes (for those tired feet).
- Pair of bifocals from Goodwill.
- Brochures from Forest Lawn Cemetery.

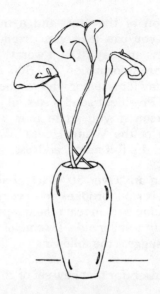

- Large-print book.
- Jar of Porcelana for your age spots.
- Senior discount bus application.
- A copy of *I'd Rather be Forty than Pregnant* ($3.95, Contemporary Books, Chicago, IL: 1984).

ANNIVERSARY PARTY

An anniversary is the perfect time to bring together family and friends for a celebration. You can throw an anniversary party for yourselves and ask your friends to bring "memories" instead of gifts. Or you can host a special anniversary party for a favorite couple and make it a gala event.

You might want to re-create the wedding—or create the wedding they never had—complete with wedding cake, photographer, even a minister or justice of the peace. Or you might want to bring back the "good old days," when the couple were young and in love, by providing music from the teenage years—the Big Band sound or be-bop—and set the atmosphere to fit the year they were married.

Another nice idea that's easy on everyone is to chip in and rent a cabin in a nearby resort town and hold the party there. The money contributed toward the party could go for cleanup as well, which makes for an easy finale.

Any year may be celebrated, but the big ones—fifth, tenth, twentieth, twenty-fifth, and fiftieth—are the most popular milestones.

There are traditional themes for anniversaries that you may want to design your party around. Here's a list for easy reference:

First Year   Paper
Second Year   Cotton
Third Year   Leather
Fourth Year   Books/Fruits & Flowers
Fifth Year   Wood
Sixth Year   Iron
Seventh Year   Wool/ Copper
Eighth Year   Bronze
Ninth Year   Pottery
Tenth Year   Tin/Aluminum
Eleventh Year   Steel
Twelfth Year   Linen/Silk
Thirteenth Year   Lace

Fourteenth Year   Ivory
Fifteenth Year   Crystal
Twentieth Year   China
Twenty-fifth Year   Silver
Thirtieth Year   Pearl
Thirty-fifth Year   Coral/ Jade
Fortieth Year   Ruby
Forty-fifth Year   Sapphire
Fiftieth Year   Gold
Fifty-fifth Year   Emerald
Sixtieth Year   Diamond, yellow
Seventy-fifth Year   Diamond Jubilee

We've got a few ideas ahead to help you get started on creating a memorable anniversary party, and you might want to borrow some ideas from the Wedding Shower, too.

INVITATIONS

Here are some unusual ways to invite guests to your anniversary party. And don't forget to check the Wedding Shower for more ideas on creative invitations.

● Purchase some inexpensive plastic champagne glasses and write the names of the honored guests on them. Some craft stores sell a liquid "silver" you could use to write the names. On the opposite side of the glass, or on the bottom,

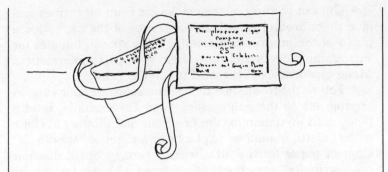

write the party details. Tie a small wisp of artificial flowers or bells with white ribbon around the stem and mail glasses in a small box, or have them hand delivered.

• Cut out double hearts from red tagboard and write party information inside. Punch a small hole at the top and tie on red or white ribbon. Mail to guests.

• Cut out two white doves and add party details on the backs. Connect the doves with a thin strand of white ribbon and drop in envelope with white confetti at the bottom.

• Buy tiny bride-and-groom figures at the cake or party store and tie card with party details to figures. Mail.

• Write out a marriage certificate on parchment paper. Fill in party details instead of wedding details. Roll into tube and tie with white and red ribbon. Mail in cardboard tube.

• Have your invitations printed by a professional printer to look like an actual wedding invitation. This is especially classy for a twenty-fifth or fiftieth anniversary.

• Borrow a picture of the couple as young bride and groom and a picture of them today. Make photocopies, then use the bride-and-groom or newlywed photo for the front of your invitation and the photo as they are today on the inside with your party details.

• Buy postcard reproductions of Grant Wood's "American Gothic" and write party details on the back.

- Cut out pictures of famous lovers from magazines and glue them around a card. In the center of the card, glue a photo of the anniversary couple. Draw speech bubbles for surrounding lovers and have them give party information. Make photocopies of the card to send to guest.

- Follow the traditional theme and send out an invitation appropriate to the anniversary year. For example, send a fancy card invitation for the first year and fill the envelope with confetti; a small wood plaque or a sheet of "wood-look" Contact paper for the fifth; wrap a card in tinfoil that has been wrinkled, smoothed, and colored with felt-tip pen for the tenth; send a small fake crystal for the fifteenth; make a Chinese fan or write an invitation on a small Chinese paper lantern for the twentieth; use silver paper with silver stars to write your party information for the twenty-fifth; make formal invitations on white paper using gold printing or ink and wrap the card in gold wrapping paper, then tie with gold cord for the fiftieth.

DECORATIONS

Just as for the Wedding Shower, you'll want to create a romantic atmosphere for the honored guests. Here are some additional ideas for making your party room romantic.

- Cut out red hearts from tagboard and tie them to the ceiling with red ribbon. Or use the dove theme and tie white doves and lovebirds to the ceiling with white ribbon.

- Buy or rent pots of flowers and plants and fill the room with blossoms and greenery. Tie large pink, red, and white bows to the plants. Hang little white dove cutouts and red heart cutouts to the branches with thread.

- Enlarge a photograph of the couple and hang it on the wall. Ask friends and relatives about important dates in the couple's life together and write them down on heart-shaped

cards and surround the poster with the cards. Then draw a line from the poster to the cards using colored yarn to create a history of the couple's romantic past.

• Make a decorative time line of the couple's romance from pictures gathered from family and friends. Line the photos along one wall, with romantic or funny captions underneath.

• Re-create the couple's courtship period with items from their teenage years. Make copies of old newspaper headlines the day they met and the day they were married. Hang posters of them as young lovers. Have the guests dress in the style of their courtship years. Play appropriate music from the era.

• Spray paint your centerpiece with silver or gold paint to make it look dazzling for the silver or gold anniversaries. Or just give it a sweep with the spray paint to gild the edges a bit.

• Decorate your room using the traditional theme suggestions. For example: For the first—use paper flowers, paper tablecloths, paper plates and napkins, paper cutouts, paper centerpiece, and paper accessories. For the fifth—decorate with wooden plaques, use wooden bowls and serving pieces, set the food on wooden tables or barrels, paint names on wooden scraps for place markers. For the tenth—cover the table with foil, wrap all the gifts in foil, use any kind of metal serving containers, add metal accessories like candle holders, serving spoons, and candy bowls. For the fifteenth—rent, borrow, or use your own crystal to serve the food and drink, hang small crystals from the ceiling, fill crystal bowls with "crystal" candy. For the twentieth—keep your china theme with Chinese accents, fortune cookies, and incense. Use your best china to serve the food. For the twenty-fifth—use all silver serving pieces. Hang silver stars and silver bells from the ceiling. For the fiftieth—fill the room with golden flowers (daffodils, mums, yellow roses). Use a lace tablecloth over gold paper wrap. Hang gold wedding bands (or gold stars and bells) from the ceiling.

GAMES

"The Newlywed Game" from the Wedding Shower would be perfect for your Anniversary Party. But one of the best games we've played was an individually designed "Personal Trivia" game. Borrowing on the trivia rage, we wrote questions pertinent to the group of friends attending the party. Not only did we have a great evening quizzing each other on little-known facts, we learned a lot more about our friends than we ever cared to know! Here's how to play:

Personal Trivia Game

Several days before the party, call each of your guests and ask them some questions about their background. (We've written some questions below that worked well for us, but you may think of some others.) Tell them not to discuss these questions or their answers with anyone. If you're inviting a large group (eight or more people) jot down about fifteen questions/answers per person. If it's a smaller group, you'll need more questions. Cut some brightly colored paper into small cards and write the questions on one side of the cards and the answers on the other. Shuffle the cards before you begin the game.

Depending on the size of the group, divide into teams or play individually. You can use one of your "Trivial Pursuit" game boards, or simply go around the room drawing cards and asking questions, and keep track of points. If it's your turn to read a question, look at the answer first and make sure it is not a question about the person who must answer. Just replace that card and select another. Note: You, as the host, will know all the answers, since you wrote all the questions. Nevertheless, its great fun watching the group struggle for answers, make mistakes, and enjoy the game.

Here are some questions we used at our Trivia game and that worked well, but you may think of others. The "Phone" question is what you ask on the telephone before the party. The "Card" question is an example of how you might write it on the card.

1. Phone: What were you doing when you met your spouse?

Card: When Marion Thatch met John she was working as (a) a forest ranger, (b) a census taker, (c) a pooper scooper, or (d) a belly dancer?

2. Phone: What's the most unusual job you've ever had during your marriage?

Card: Which one of us actually worked as a gravedigger?

3. Phone: Have you won any awards in the past or had some king of honorable mention for something?

Card: Which one of us carried the title Miss Hog Caller of 1978?

4. Phone: How did you meet your partner?

Card: Where did Bob meet Anne? (a) at McDonalds, (b) in the men's room, (c) at the unemployment office, (d) over a CB radio.

5. Phone: Where did you go on your first date?

Card: Where did Gary take Rikki on their first date? (a) his apartment, (b) his bedroom, (c) the backseat of his car, (d) home.

---

6. Phone: Where was your most unusual vacation?

Card: Who in this crowd spent three weeks at a fat farm?

7. Phone: What are your pets' names?

Card: Who named their pet goldfish Fifi?

8. Phone: What was your maiden name?

Card: Who was formerly known as Miss Bilgebottom?

9. Phone: Where was your "First Time"?

Card: Which one of us "did it" for the first time on the Space Mountain ride at Disneyland?"

10. Phone: What is your pet name for your partner?

Card: Who in this room is usually referred to in private as Snookie-woozie-poo?

11. Phone: Where were you born?

Card: Which historical town does Tom claim as his birthplace? (a) Muscogie, Illinois, (b) Gorky Park, (c) Yuba City, California, (d) Ellis Island.

12. Phone: What's the strangest adventure you ever had?

Card: Name the person here who escaped from a Russian gulag.

Here are some other activities you might want to consider for your anniversary party:

• Have everyone bring a photo of the couple, along with an amusing story. Mount the photos on the wall and at game time ask each guest to tell an anecdote about the couple. Place all the pictures in an album after the party to give to the couple.

• Video tape interviews with all the guests during the party asking how they met the couple and asking them to relate a special memory about the couple. Play it back for the crowd and give it to the couple as a gift at the end of the party.

• Ask each guest to come prepared with a question to ask the happy couple relating to something that happened in the past. For example, if the guest went on vacation with the couple, she might ask "What happened in Fresno on

July 19, 1967?" If the couple can remember, they get a small prize—maybe a gag gift.

• See if you can surreptitiously borrow slides from the couple's home collection and pick out some of the funniest ones. Give a slide show and ask the couple to explain each picture. Or give your own funny version of what's going on in the picture.

REFRESHMENTS

One of the nicest touches I've seen at an anniversary party was a small version of a wedding cake. It set the mood, served as a stunning centerpiece, and fed all the guests. And it doesn't have to be expensive if you keep it simple and small.

Again, many of the refreshments in the Wedding Shower would be appropriate at the Anniversary Party. Or try something elegant like cream puffs filled with white chocolate mousse. Or fill a graham cracker crust with a small carton of frozen raspberries, thawed. Then cover with a mixture of your favorite cheesecake recipe, and top with chocolate sauce that will harden when refrigerated. Decorate with whipped cream rosettes and fresh raspberries.

Pour pink champagne or make a fruit punch to serve with the fancy desserts.

PRIZES/GIFTS/FAVORS

If the guests need gifts suggestions, refer to the traditional theme list for ideas. You might also recommend a romantic dinner for two; sexy nightwear; theater tickets; tickets for a local boat cruise; a basket of wine, cheese, and French bread; a romantic album and massage oil; or a night on the town.

If you have game winners, award a bottle of pink champagne, a small game of trivia, a romantic album, a small bouquet of flowers, a romance novel, or something from the general list in the introduction.

And send the guests home with something romantic, like a single red rose, a small corsage, some envelopes of bubble bath, or a split of champagne.

Here's a special idea for a couple celebrating a fiftieth anniversary or above. The President of the United States will send the couple a personal anniversary card if you write to the "Greetings Office of the White House, Washington, D. C. 20500," four weeks before the anniversary date. Be sure to include the full name of the couple, the address, and the occasion.

FAMILY AND OTHER REUNIONS

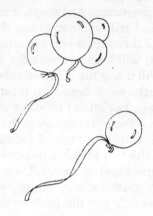

Reunions are a great way to gather together relatives, old friends, past neighbors, army buddies, and school chums.

I attended my first family reunion last summer, a little reluctant to go since it was my husband's family and I knew very few of his long-lost relatives. But I came away feeling as if I'd known them all my life—that was the spirit with which the reunion was given.

Reunions call for special planning since many of the guests no longer live close by. The host may have to make arrangements for the out-of-towners at local hotels, or clear out a large room for countless sleeping bags. This, along with numerous other details, can be overwhelming.

So before you begin, ask another reunion member who lives nearby to help out with the organization, party, and cleanup. The more help you can get, the smoother your reunion will run.

One of the best ideas for planning our family reunion was the setting up of individual committees. Each attending family was assigned a reunion task. For example, some organized and assigned food, some prepared the games, some were in charge of entertainment, some helped with the preparation of the house or party site, and some were assigned to clean up. Your reunion may also require someone to handle the invitations and maps, another to cover the serving of food, and still another to see that everyone has accommodations. All reunions will benefit from this type of division of labor. It will help you with the burden of hosting the reunion and will make the other members feel involved.

Picnics or potlucks work best with most reunion parties. Groups can get together ahead to make up the food, or all can bring their contributions the day of the party. You might also consider meeting at a central location—somewhere halfway between the two farthest points—and have guests all stay at the same hotel or motel. Do your partying at a local park, which makes things easier on everyone. End with a pancake breakfast in the park on the last day before the group heads home.

Your reunion might also take on a theme each year. Perhaps one year the theme is memories, while another time you'll want to focus on reacquaintances. Other ideas might be "New Members" (a focus on the introduction and welcome of new family members through marriage or birth), "What's New?" (a theme to bring everyone up-to-date on recent accomplishments and activities), "Predictions" (everyone predicts a future for each reunion member, then all check back in a number of years to see what happened), or pick out a theme from the Miscellaneous Party section and turn your reunion into a "Snow Bunny" ski party, a *Gone With the Wind* garden party, or a "Texas barbecue."

So whatever type of get-together you're planning—family reunion, old neighborhood reunion, even high school reunion—here are some tips and suggestions to help make it your best ever.

INVITATIONS

There are lots of ways to create unusual reunion invitations to send to your relatives, neighbors, or school pals.

Family Reunion

• Photocopy a picture of your own family and fold it into a card. Write the details of the reunion inside.

• Collect a photo of the oldest family member and the youngest. Cut them out and tape them to a folded sheet of paper to make a card. Unfold the paper and photocopy it, then refold it and write your reunion information inside. If your photocopy store does double-sided printing, write the party details inside first, then photocopy. You might mention something about getting everyone together between "granny" and "baby."

• Cut out a family tree trunk from brown construction paper and glue it onto a white sheet of paper. Write party details around tree as leaves.

• Make a detailed family tree with all the family member names as leaves. Put question marks for missing information of relatives and ask members to fill in the blanks and bring them along to the reunion.

• If your family has a sign or symbol, or your last name has another meaning, such as Blackstone or Nightingale, create the sign on the card. Or use the family crest if you have one.

• Photocopy a geneology chart and use it as the cover for your invitation.

• Draw a 5″ × 5″ quilt pattern and use it for your invitation. Ask each family to create a quilt square symbolizing something about their family, and bring it along to the reunion (see Games/Activities).

• Make a mini-family album from tagboard and write reunion information inside.

- In your invitation, ask your family members to bring along photos to share with the group (see Decorations).
- Make "Secret Pal" invitations. Assign one family member to be a secret pal to another family member and to be creative in providing that pal with special treats, notes, small gifts, surprises, and so on. It's especially nice if a young person and an older person are assigned to each other (but not the *same* ones for each other).
- Cut out a map of your area, photocopy it, and glue it onto an invitation. Draw a line from your town to the edge of the card. When you open card, have the line continue to a photocopied map of your family's town. Write details at the bottom.
- Collect baby pictures from some of the older relatives and photocopy them for the front of the invitation with "Guess who?" as a caption. Reveal their identities at the reunion.
- Write some family trivia questions on the invitation to be filled in before the reunion. Try to make the questions obscure—little-known facts will be the most surprising.

Old Neighborhood Reunion

- Have an artist draw the old neighborhood, labeled with each family name, and use it for the front of your invitation.
- Trace a map of the city, county, state, or country and label each new home where an old neighbor has moved with a yellow flag. Draw lines from all the new homes to the old neighborhood.
- Draw some simple mailboxes with all the names of the old neighbors and their new addresses on the front of the invitation. Inside, draw one large mailbox and list all the names again.
- Photocopy pictures of the old gang to use for the invitation. Write funny captions under each person.

School Reunion

● Photocopy a picture of the school and place it on the front of the invitation with the name of the school and the years your class attended, such as "Del Valle High School, 1961–1965." Inside, photocopy a picture of an old shack and write "Del Valle High School, after 1965."

● Begin your invitation with trivia questions, such as "Who was voted class clown?" "Who was expelled for stealing the school mascot?" and other questions that will jog the memory and get people in the mood.

● Send out invitations in the school colors, with the school mascot on the cover.

● Pick out several funny pictures from the yearbook and photocopy them on the cover of the invitation with the caption "Where are they now?" Inside, print recent pictures of the same people with funny captions, such as "Head cheerleader at Herman's Automotive School," "Serving five to ten for not getting a haircut."

● Contact some teachers from your school and take recent photos of them. Use them for the front of your invitation with funny captions, such as phrases they typically used in class.

DECORATIONS

If the party will be mostly outdoors, keep the decorations simple—just set a welcoming table with loads of food and you won't need much else. Here are a few extra touches for both indoor buffets and outdoor picnics.

Family Reunion

● If you're having a sit-down dinner for the whole crew, set up lengths of table covered with Americana print tablecloths (or anything that's reminiscent of your family's heritage).

● Put a special gift for each guest at each place setting. For example, a nephew's favorite comic book, an aunt's favorite flower, a grandmother's favorite tea. Or place photographs of each family member at each place.

● If you've saved mementos from past get-togethers, place them around the house with notes describing the memory attached.

● If you have a collection of photographs of all the family members, place them around the house with descriptions.

● Have T-shirts made with the names of all the family members printed on the shirts and the date of the family reunion. This makes a wonderful keepsake, and if you have several printed at a time they won't be terribly expensive. You might request money to cover the cost when you send the invitations.

● Make a large family tree from construction paper and hang on the wall. Cut out colorful leaves and write the names of the family members on them. As they arrive, have them add their leaves to the tree in family groups, or hang them before the guests arrive.

● Ask all your family members to bring old family albums to share. Set them out on a special table for all to look at during the reunion.

● With a very large crowd you may need name tags. Write the names of families on separate colors so the relatives can tell who belongs to which family.

● Have a large sheet of paper on the wall with the family name at the top, written in fancy colorful letters. Have each guest sign in and write a word of greeting or a special event that has occurred during the year. Read the sheet aloud after all have arrived, or let the relatives read it silently at their leisure.

● As each family arrives, assign a relative to take them in a room and make a silhouette of their heads, or a full body outline on a large sheet of paper. Cut out head or figure and attach to the walls as completed. These make wonderful decorations and lasting memories to share each year.

Old Neighborhood Reunion

● If at all possible, have the party in the old neighborhood. If no one lives there any more, perhaps there's a park nearby, a favorite restaurant, or a hotel you can use.
● Tie large yellow ribbons around all the trees, posts, and so on, to welcome the guests.
● Have neighbors bring pictures of new homes to put along the walls.
● Put pictures of people from the old neighborhood around the room.
● Decorate the party room to look like the old neighborhood. Cover large sheets of paper with drawings of old landmarks, houses, corner stores, and so on. Hang the large sheets on the walls to transform the room.

School Reunion

● Have T-shirts made with the roster of all classmates.
● Hang blowups of some funny pictures from the yearbook.
● Decorate in the school colors.
● Hang signs reminiscent of school cheers—"Beat Cal" or "Stop Stanford."
● Hang "before" and "after" photos of the class officers, cheerleaders, and other highly visible students. Place their graduation pictures next to current pictures.
● Re-create the senior prom theme.
● Play music from your teenage years.

GAMES/ACTIVITIES

Most of the time during reunions is spent with the adults catching up on news while the kids run off and play. But if you'd like to have a few organized activities, here are some designed just for family reunions, but most can be adapted for neighborhood, school, and other reunions.

● If many of the family members are unacquainted, play a variation on "Get-Acquainted Bingo" in the Christmas Party (see page 79). My friend's father introduced this game at his large family reunion and it helped break the ice for those long-lost relatives who felt out of touch. It also gets everyone mingling and helps them catch up on the latest news.

● Collect little-known facts about each family member before the reunion (or do it discreetly during the reunion). Write each fact down with the name next to it. During activity time, gather the family members and read off the little-known fact. Ask them to guess who it is.

● Gather the group and have each family member state three things: (1) What do you like best about your family? (2) What's a funny or unusual thing your family does? (3) What's the best thing that ever happened to your family? This is a great way to get to know one another better.

● During the afternoon, ask family members to write down five of their worst dislikes on a 3 × 5-inch card. During dinner, read the cards one at a time, and ask the group to guess which relative it is. Substitute dislikes for likes, memories, fantasies, dreams, or anything else you think your group would enjoy.

● If you ask each of your relatives to bring a quilt square, join together and have a quilting bee. Assemble the squares while you talk over old times and catch up on the family gossip. When the quilt comes together, hang it on the wall and bring it to each family gathering. If you make this a yearly tradition, choose a theme each year and allow different family members to keep the quilts until the next reunion. These quilts make lasting heirlooms for the family heritage.

- Ask each family to bring a family photo to the reunion and place them all in an album. Bring the albums to the gatherings each year to share.
- Collect photos at each party and put them into an album. Bring the album each year.
- Have the relatives guess which silhouettes belong to which family members.
- Collect bits of family trivia and make up colorful trivia question cards. For example, if you learned that Uncle Ed won $20 in the lottery, turn that into a question—"Who won $20 in the lottery last week?" Tape the question cards around the house and let the relatives discover them and write down their answers. When all have had a chance to guess, read the cards aloud and have the subjects of the trivia questions give the right answers.
- Make a video tape of each family member describing how he or she is related to the family.
- Ask each family member to bring along a family memory and share them one at a time during the dinner.
- Have an awards ceremony after dinner, with prizes or small trophies for such achievements as: Who's the oldest? Who's the youngest? Who's the longest married? Who came the farthest? Who made the best dessert? Who's the sweetest? Who worked the hardest? Who arrived the latest? Who ate the most? Who's here for the first time?
- Have one or two adults take turns being in charge of a few organized games for the kids—baseball, kickball, soccer, kick the can, badminton, kite flying, and so on.
- Start a new tradition with an "Elder Story." Have the oldest member of the family tell or write and read aloud the story of his or her life.
- Bring a song to share and make up a family song book.
- When everyone's tired from the busy day, show home movies from different families.

REFRESHMENTS

If you're hosting a large gathering, the easiest party style is a potluck buffet. Make a list of food categories—appetizers (snacks, chips and dips, finger foods), salads (green, gelatin, potato, pasta, and fruit), main dishes (meats, casseroles), breads (rolls, muffins, crackers), fruits and vegetables (hot, cold), desserts (cakes, pies, cookies, brownies), beverages (beer, wine, soda, milk, fruit juice, water)—then ask each guest to bring a favorite dish from an assigned category. When the foods arrive, label them with the name of the dish and the cook's name, and refrigerate all the foods that may spoil. Serve buffet style with sturdy paper plates.

If you're planning to make all the food, here are a few suggestions for feeding the masses easily:

● Order a long poorboy sandwich (up to six feet) from the local deli. The cost is reasonable and the giant loaf makes an attractive conversation piece. Serve with a large, sharp serrated knife so guests can cut away lengths of the sandwich at their leisure.

● Have a pasta feast. Days before the event, cook up pots of various Italian sauces (marinara, clam, Alfredo, and so on), or ask a few guests to bring a favorite pasta sauce. At mealtime, cook up four large pots of four different pastas (spaghetti, fettuccine, corkscrew, tortellini, or any favorite pasta). Let guests mix and match pastas and sauces. Serve with loaves of French bread and a large green salad.

● Cook up a large pot of chili and serve it with corn bread and a green salad. Have sliced watermelon for dessert.

● Have a do-it-yourself shish kebab cook-out. Cut steak or chicken into cubes, place in bowls, and marinate overnight. Cut up green pepper, onion, cherry tomatoes, mushrooms, corn-on-the-cob, zucchini, and pineapple and place in individual bowls. Give each guest a skewer and let them

create and then cook their own shish kebab. Serve with rice and salad.

● Serve taco shells and fixings and let the gang fill them as desired.

● Ask each guest to bring a boxed lunch in a decorated shoe box, basket, or bandanna. Place all the boxed lunches on the table and draw numbers or bid on the different boxes, without revealing the contents. If you auction them off, use the money for games, prizes, or other shared expense. If the boxes are decorated, award a prize for most beautiful, funniest, most creative, and so on.

● Have a guest bring a favorite family dish to the reunion, along with photocopies of the recipe. Pass out the recipes in the form of a cookbook to go home with each family.

● Serve a stunning and unique "patchwork cake" for dessert. On the reunion invitation, ask each guest to bring a piece of cake, 8 inches square, and decorated, with the name of the contributors added on top. As guests arrive, take cakes and place right next to each other on a large table to form one enormous patchwork cake. The cake makes a wonderful centerpiece—don't forget to take a picture of it.

PRIZES/GIFTS/FAVORS

If you have an awards ceremony, be sure to have some small trophies or gifts on hand. Here are some ideas:

- A T-shirt with the names of all the reunion members makes a lasting keepsake.
- Have a group picture made. You can send out copies to all the participants after the party is over. At the next reunion you can enlarge the picture and use it as part of your decorations.
- A photocopy of the family tree.
- Have bumper stickers or pins made up with some special slogan from your group—"I'm a Member of the Whozits Family," "Smokerise Court—a Chip off the Old Block," "I Survived the Class of '65."
- Give everyone address books and have them fill in the information before they leave the party.
- Stationery to keep everyone in touch.

CHRISTMAS PARTY

The Christmas holidays offer a perfect time to host a party—from the traditional Christmas Eve tree-trimming event, attended only by family members, to the gala celebrations with lots of friends, food, and festivities.

You might want to have friends over for a candlelight dinner party and a quiet gift exchange. Or have the relatives over on Christmas Eve for carols and hot cider, or take your carolers on a stroll through the neighborhood or local convalescent hospital. Maybe a get-together before or after church services, with a buffet dinner and gift opening, would be right for your party plans.

Many people like to host an open house during the holiday season—an afternoon of seeing old friends and serving little goodies. You might enjoy having close friends in one evening for warm drinks, candles, and Christmas music. Or keep it basic and have the popular Christmas cocktail party, maybe with a theme or tradition each year.

Gather your friends together for a gift-making party—an informal get-together to share ideas and materials, to work and talk, to eat and drink. If you make this a regular event, you'll soon have enough gifts to open your own holiday boutique.

I start planning my annual Christmas party a month before my chosen date. This way I enjoy the preparations as well as the party, which is half the fun.

One of our traditions is to include an optional "cookie exchange" during the party. We tell the guests to bring three dozen of their favorite cookies if they're so inclined, and at the end of the evening they can circle around the cookie table and collect three dozen assorted cookies to take home for the family. (Make that two dozen to take home if you're going to let them eat some during the party! Otherwise you'll need a sign—"No nibbling!") It's a fun way to share Christmas joy without going to a lot of trouble, and the cookie table makes a festive display during the party.

My friend Lucy has begun a nice tradition at her annual Christmas party, too. She hosts an "ornament exchange." She asks each guest to bring a tree ornament to the party, nicely wrapped and unlabeled. During the party she gathers the guests around the tree and has them each select a number written on a small piece of paper. The guest who picks number one gets to select the first wrapped ornament, followed by two, and so on. Each guest unwraps the gift for all to see, and adds it to his or her own collection.

Your Christmas party theme is usually that—Christmas. But if you'd like to take the theme a step further, you can decorate the house each year with a little different style, just like Macy's department store. Each year Macy's windows are visited by thousands of window-shoppers who look forward to viewing the different Christmas themes. One year we watched elves creating toys in the workshop, another year it was the story of Rudolph the Red-Nosed Reindeer. The most memorable was "Snow in San Francisco," with miniatures of the city's buildings covered with soft artificial snow—an uncommon sight in our picturesque city by the bay. If you have the time, energy, and imagination, why not create a winter wonderland or country Christmas in your living room, too?

INVITATIONS

There are so many ways to invite your guests to your Christmas party. Here are a few I have used in the past.

● Make your invitation out of cookie dough. Cut sugar cookies into circles, poke a small hole at the top to run string through, bake, and decorate with tubes of frosting. Write your party information on the cookie and allow to dry. Run red string through the hole to make the cookie look like an ornament and place cookie in tissue paper in a small box. Wrap with Christmas wrap and hand-deliver.

● Write your party details on a white card with red ink, drop in flat box, and wrap with Christmas paper. Send through the mail.

● Buy six-inch candy canes and twist pipe cleaner around top to form antlers for reindeer (see illustration). Glue on plastic eyes from hobby store as shown. Tie a card to candy cane with party details and hand-deliver.

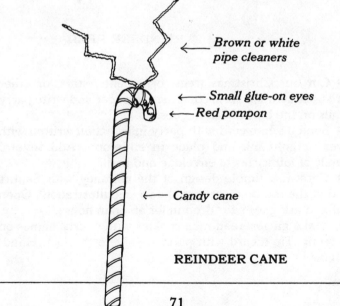

← *Brown or white pipe cleaners*

← *Small glue-on eyes*
← *Red pompon*

← *Candy cane*

REINDEER CANE

• Buy eight-inch candy canes and brown felt. Cut out reindeer heads as shown (see illustration) and glue to form head. Glue on eyes and red pompon nose. Attach party information and hand-deliver.

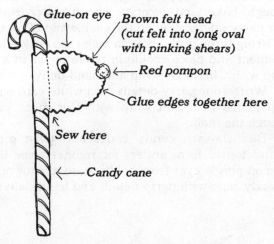

Glue-on eye

Brown felt head
(cut felt into long oval
with pinking shears)

Red pompon

Glue edges together here

Sew here

Candy cane

REINDEER HEAD

• Cut out Christmas trees, ornaments, stars, or other Christmas symbols from construction paper and write party details on the back. Mail to guests.
• Send a white card with party information written with silver or gold ink and place in envelope. Add several strands of foil icicles to envelope and mail.
• Copy the simple design of the chimney with Santa's hand at the top on a card, as shown (see illustration). Open card and ask guests to "drop in for an open house."
• Make gingerbread man cookies with guests' names on the front. Tie a card with party details to the foot. Hand-deliver.

Invite guests to drop in with a picture like this one.

● Make baker's clay from 4 cups flour, 1 cup salt, 1¾ cups water. Add several drops of red or green food coloring and knead well. Roll out dough and cut into stars or other Christmas shapes with cookie cutters. Poke holes at the top for string and bake on foil at 250°F for 2 to 3 hours. Write party details on the back with felt-tip pen and mail or deliver to guests.

● Cut tagboard into star shapes, cover with foil, and write party details on top.

● Buy small poinsettia plants and tie party details to each. Hand-deliver to guests.

● Write party details on white card, tie thin red and green ribbon around fold, and attach a small bell. Mail in envelope.

● Tie some ribbon around a slip of mistletoe along with a card with party details and mail in envelope to guests.

● Cut out felt ornaments, decorate with liquid embroidery (available at fabric stores), and mail to guests with party details written on the back in felt-tip pen.

● Cut out construction paper or felt in shape of holly leaves with red berries and write party information on the back. Mail to guests.

● Reproduce a favorite Christmas poem for front of invitation and write information inside.

- Reproduce a favorite Christmas scene from a holiday book and send as invitation.
- Cut out a wreath from green felt. Glue tiny red felt circles around the wreath, tie a thin red ribbon at the top, and mount the wreath on tagboard. Write party details around the wreath. Mail to guests.
- Purchase small inexpensive ornaments and attach party invitation. Hand-deliver or mail in small padded envelope or box.

DECORATIONS

The decorations for your Christmas party should be easy—just unpack the box in the attic marked "Christmas" and transform your home into Santa's workshop. Here are a few more ideas you might want to add to get your home ready for the holiday celebration:

- Use red and green felt to cover tabletops, mantels, and counters. It's easier to use than fabric because there's no hemming needed. You can also use the felt for place mats, coasters, and as a skirt for the tree.
- Hang fresh boughs of pine on the mantel, on the door, and along the bathroom counter.
- Place candy canes all around the house as decorations.
- String your own cranberry/popcorn garlands to hang on the tree, to drape along the mantel, to outline a window, or to frame your table setting.
- Tie mistletoe and holly with red and green ribbon and hang at the front doorway, in the kitchen, and in the bathroom over the toilet for a laugh.
- Buy some inexpensive poinsettia plants and place them on the fireplace, at the door, on the tables, in groups on the floor, or on the mantel.
- Small colorful Christmas stockings, Santas, candy

canes, and ornaments look terrific taped or pinned to bedroom doors or other doors throughout the house. Or think of some creative places to put them to surprise your guests.

• Buy bags of polyester fiberfill or angel hair and drape it over tables and shelves to make it look as if you had an indoor blizzard. Then set your decorations and food on top.

• Buy a roll of colored foil wrapping paper and tape or staple it securely to two large sheets of tagboard that, when fit together, are the size of your front door. Buy bags of hard, wrapped Christmas candy—peppermints, butterballs, sourballs, red and green kisses, and so on—and glue or tape them to the paper. Allow glue to dry, then staple the cardboard sections to the door to make a brilliant and exciting welcome for your guests. (Promise the neighborhood kids the "door" after Christmas and they'll leave it alone.)

• Wrap the door in Christmas foil and "tie" on a big red ribbon bow to make the door look like a giant present.

• Make garlands for the tree and the mantel from hard, wrapped candies. Buy a variety of candies and tie the twisted ends to another end of a candy with red and green curling ribbon. Curl ribbon and continue until you have the length you want.

• With a square cardboard box and an extra sheet of cardboard folded in half to form a roof, make a "gingerbread" house by taping the roof section to the square box. Cover the box with foil wrap, then glue cellophane- and foil-wrapped candies onto the wrap, in patterns, until the entire surface is covered. Set on angel hair.

• String tiny, blinking colored lights throughout the *inside* of your house—on the mantel, around the windows, on the bookcase.

• Buy a large supply of votive candles and holders and set them throughout the house.

• Make a teddy ornament tree. Buy a small Christmas tree and set it on the table. Make enough baker's clay teddy bears for all your guests, using illustration as a guide. Stick a paper clip into the top of his head to form hook. After baked and hard, paint with brown acrylic paint, adding detail with

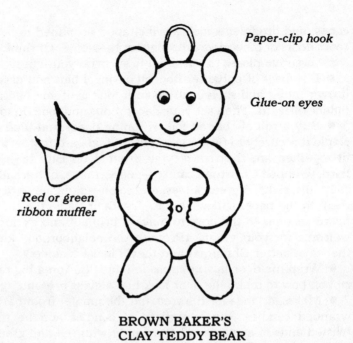

Paper-clip hook

Glue-on eyes

Red or green
ribbon muffler

**BROWN BAKER'S
CLAY TEDDY BEAR**

black paint. Tie on thin ribbon and tie bear to tree. These cute ornaments can be given out at the end of the party as gifts, prizes, or favors.

• Make small candy-cane reindeer with pipe cleaners and hang on tree (see Invitations). Give to guests at end of party.

• Make larger candy-cane reindeer and set reindeer in a tall canister or bowl so that face is out and hook is inside. Fill bowl or can with goodies. Give to guest to take home to their children at the end of the party.

• Buy or collect little jars. (Baby food jars full of baby food are usually cheaper than anything else I've found! Buy the ones filled with juice, empty them into a container, and keep in refrigerator for the kids.) Cover the lids with baker's clay, pressing fork around sides to make a finished design. Bake at 250° F for 2 to 3 hours, until hard. Glue red and green jelly beans on the lid and fill the small jars with jelly beans. Tie a ribbon around the neck and set around tables and shelves. Give to guests as favors, gifts, or prizes. An easier way might be to paint the lids red or green with enamel paint and glue a cute little Santa (available at the hobby store) on the top.

● Sew some fur fabric or felt as shown in illustration to form Santa's legs. Hang in fireplace if you're not having a fire so that Santa looks as if he's coming down the chimney.

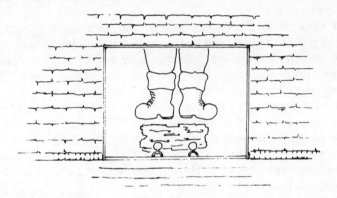

SANTA'S LEGS   *Cut leg pattern from red felt, boots from black felt, boot tops from white felt or fiberfill. Hang from inside of fireplace.*

● Place some of your garlands along mantels, bookcases, tables, and counters, and hang some ornaments from the ceiling or along the walls.

● Dress up as Santa, Mrs. Claus, or an elf. Wear bells, or attach bells to all your guests as they walk in the door.

● Make up a batch of sugar cookies and roll to ½ inch thick. With a sharp knife, cut out letters to spell a holiday greeting—"Merry Christmas," "Joy to the World," "Bah, Humbug!" Bake cookies according to directions and let cool. Outline around letters with decorator tube in red or green frosting. Add a tiny holly leaf and three little berries on the corners of the letters and lay out on tables or prop up along windowsills or the mantel.

• Dress tables in inexpensive Christmas pattern fabric from the fabric store. Buy two table lengths, cut them in half, and sew them together along the sides to form table-cloths.

• Make elf hats from red and green felt for all your guests. Attach a pompon at the top, along with a small bell, and top your guests as they enter.

• Line a wall with your Christmas card collection from several years.

• Play your Christmas albums or turn on the radio; usually there are several stations playing holiday music.

• Let the kids paint your windows full of Santas, rein-deers, presents, trees, and elves, using poster paint. Or spray your windows with "snow," using a lace doily for a stencil. Or cut out your own snowflakes from white paper and tape them on the windows.

• Make a "stained glass" window by designing a Christ-mas picture, outlining the design with black felt or con-struction paper on your chosen window, and filling in the spaces with colored cellophane.

• Hire Santa to make a surprise visit to hand out the gifts.

GAMES/ACTIVITIES

Christmas parties don't require much in the way of games or activities—most of your guests simply enjoy meeting new people, seeing old friends, and sharing good cheer.

Unfortunately, some people don't mingle well, are timid about meeting new friends, and are shy about introducing themselves to strangers. We offer several games to help people get acquainted, to get them moving out of their small groups, and to set them at ease with a roomful of strange people.

Get-Acquainted Bingo

Although this game took some time in preparation, it was well worth it. Friends are still talking about the great time they had at our last Christmas party. And many of those friends are people who do not like the typical cocktail parties.

Cut green and red paper into 3 × 4-inch cards, one for each guest. And with a pencil, draw a grid dividing each card into six squares, as shown in illustration. Cover with clear Contact paper on both sides. Place five Christmas stickers on the back of the card and write the name of one guest on the top middle square of the front. Repeat for all guests. On the front of each card, write 5 questions in the squares about other people in the group, especially people they aren't likely to know but might have something in common with. For example, "Who just had a baby?" "Who was promoted to lieutenant of the Danville Police Force last week?" "Who just returned from two months in Germany?" "Who works for a massage studio?" Be sure you use the same question on several cards and be sure you don't leave anyone out. Place five Christmas stickers on the back of each card. When the guests arrive, give them their "Get-Acquainted Bingo" cards and tell them they will receive a prize if they are able to fill up their cards by locating

1.	NAME	2.
3.	4.	5.

79

everyone connected with a question. They are to approach another guest and ask something like "Are you the one who just had the hernia operation or are you the FBI agent?" If they find someone to match the question on the card, they are to take a sticker from that person and place it over the answered question. When the guests fill all 5 spaces on their cards, award them a teddy bear ornament or a jelly bean jar (see Decorations). This game gives people a reason to meet new people and many find common interests that lead to conversation. It was the best nonthreatening, fun-filled get-acquainted game we've played.

The Match Game

Find two objects that go together—lock and key, spoon and fork, needle and thread, and so on—and collect enough pairs for all your guests. Write the names of your guests on small sticky labels and attach one to each item, thinking carefully about the pairs you are matching—no husbands and wives together, no anti-nuke supporters and nuclear engineers together, no feuding neighbors together. Then distribute the objects around the party room by taping them—*in plain sight*—to tables, walls, lamps, and chairs. During the evening, guests are to locate their names and objects and find their partners. At dinner, partners will be seated together.

Here are some additional get-acquainted ideas for your party:

• Buy a collection of candy canes. Break the candy canes in half. Give the bent half to the men and the straight half to the women as they enter the party, and have them find their match.

• Make sugar cookies in the shape of round ornaments. Cut the circles in half, using a jagged line or puzzle-like cut and separate the halves slightly. Bake according to recipe instructions. When cool, decorate like ornaments. As each guest arrives, give each a cookie half and have them find their "other half."

80

• Get a game of Christmas trivia going during the party. Write questions related to Christmas on little green Christmas tree cutouts and tape them on the walls around the house. Provide pencils and paper and, at the end of the evening, go over the questions and read the answers. Here are some of the questions we used:

    a. What is a *bûche de Noël?* (edible yule log).

    b. What do bad little boys get for Christmas? (switches and lumps of coal).

    c. Finish the song: "All I want for Christmas is . . ." (my two front teeth).

    d. Who was caught kissing Santa Claus? (mommy).

    e. How do you say Merry Christmas in Spanish and French? *(Feliz Navidad, Joyeux Noël).*

    f. Name the eight reindeer. (Dasher, Dancer, Prancer, Vixen, Comet, Cupid, Donner, and Blitzen).

    g. What did Frosty the Snowman use for a nose? (a carrot).

    h. Who wrote *The Night Before Christmas?* (Clement Clarke Moore).

    i. What exactly is the last line in the poem? (*Happy* Christmas to all, and to all a good night).

    j. What is a "Tannenbaum?" (A Christmas tree, in German.)

    k. What did the Three Wise Men bring? (gold, frankincense, and myrrh).

    l. On the twelfth day of Christmas, what did my true love give to me? (12 fiddlers fiddling, 11 lords a-leaping, 10 ladies dancing, 9 pipers piping, 8 maids a-milking, 7 swans a-swimming, 6 geese a-laying, 5 golden rings, 4 calling brids, 3 French hens, 2 turtle doves, and a partridge in a pear tree).

• Play a version of "Facts," mentioned on page 64 of the Reunion chapter, tailoring it to your group.

• Have a Christmas scavenger hunt. Divide party members into groups or couples and give them a list of Christmas-related items to locate, either in the house or in the neighborhood. You might add a candle, a religious Christmas card, some mistletoe, a Christmas cookie, a broken ornament, a burned-out tree light, a Christmas stamp, some tinsel, and some pine needles to your list.

• Ask your guests to bring an inexpensive gift for either a man or a woman, wrapped, with no name on it. Have your guests draw numbers and pick a gift in order. Or have them pick out a gift blindfolded. Or have a friend hand them a gift and if they don't like it they can exchange it with the friend.

• Don't forget the "cookie exchange" and the "ornament" exchange mentioned earlier.

REFRESHMENTS

Nothing welcomes guests better than a houseful of Christmas smells. Bake your own specialties and add a few of these quick-and-easy holiday treats:

• Have a large pot of hot mulled wine simmering on the stove. Heat red wine with several sticks of cinnamon, some cloves, and a little nutmeg. Stick cloves all over small apples or oranges and let them float in the wine. Serve to guests as they arrive.

• Have another pot of hot apple cider mixed with cranberry juice cocktail for those who don't want an alcoholic drink.

• If you are offering champagne, place a small peppermint stick inside the glass. (Here's another tip: Many guests set their drinks down and forget where they put them. As each guest arrives, write his or her initials on a small peel-and-stick circle and stick it onto the top of the base of the glass. That way guests can check to see which one is theirs.)

• For your party finale, offer cinnamon coffee. Serve mugs of coffee with a stick of cinnamon and a dollop of whipped cream on top.

• Serve "sherbet ornaments" to your party guests. With an ice cream scoop, scoop balls of raspberry, orange, and lime sherbet (and other colors if desired) onto a platter and keep in freezer until serving time. Set platter out with small plates or bowls.

• How about a do-it-yourself peppermint sundae dessert featuring peppermint ice cream and bowls of toppings—nuts, coconut, crushed candy canes, mini chocolate chips, crushed chocolate-mint sandwich cookies, chocolate sauce, and fresh mint.

• In addition to the usual array of hors d'oeuvre plates, serve an hors d'oeuvre tree at your Christmas party. Buy a large Styrofoam cone at the hobby store and cover with fancy lettuce leaves—endive and watercress are the nicest. Prepare lots of bite-size vegetables and fruits and skewer them with toothpicks into the "tree." Serve with dressing or dip.

• Serve cheese and bread cut into Christmas shapes with small cookie cutters.

• Make a red and green crudité platter with cherry tomatoes, red and green peppers, celery, lightly steamed pea pods, and red cabbage. Healthy food for the holiday feast!

• Create "petit fours presents" by baking a large yellow or white sheet cake. When cake is done and still hot, poke holes in top of cake and pour over orange juice glaze made from ¼ cup orange juice and 2 tablespoons powdered sugar mixed together. Allow to cool, then cut into small squares. Make frosting and dilute with a little water so it will pour. Pour frosting over small cakes and allow to dry. Decorate with a fine-tip tube to make "presents" by crossing two lines and adding a star or flower in the center.

• Serve your guests "champagne snowballs." Mix 2 cups lemon sherbet with ½ cup champagne and 4 ice cubes in the blender. Serve in champagne glasses with lemon twist.

• Make a simple yule log by baking a chocolate cake on a cookie sheet or jelly roll pan, icing it with white buttercream frosting, and rolling it up into a log. Frost the log with chocolate frosting, swirling the frosting to make the "bark," and top with cherry halves and chopped walnuts.

PRIZES/GIFTS/FAVORS

Every year I give my guests personalized gifts with a touch of whimsy. For example, my friend who's a cosmetics saleswoman received a bottle of cologne from a competitor, a friend who'd just returned from Hawaii got a free session in a tanning booth, and a friend who had just bought a new car deserved a bumper sticker that said "My other car is a hunk of junk."

If you make up some little gifts ahead of time, like the teddy bear ornaments and jelly bean jars, hand them out as you say good-bye to your guests. And don't forget to send home a candy-cane reindeer for the kids.

If you have an ornament or gift exchange, your guests won't be leaving empty handed. Add a small tin or plate of homemade fudge gaily wrapped in cellophane and ribbons.

But best of all, your guests will enjoy taking home their batch of three dozen assorted cookies!

And since most people get saturated with sweets and fatty foods during the holidays, why not send them home with an alternative: unsalted nuts, a loaf of homemade bread, a jar of whole figs or dates, a pomander ball, a jar of potpourri, an orange filled with clove spikes and tied in pretty ribbon for hanging, a split of wine or champagne. Wrap everything in festive paper or tie with lots of curly red and green ribbon and hand them out to your departing guests at the end of the evening.

NEW YEAR'S PARTY

Welcome the new year with a party! You can make it the traditional late-night New Year's Eve party or opt for an afternoon football and food at a New Year's Day party.

If it's New Year's Eve, you might want to begin it on the late side—8 or 9 o'clock—since you're almost guaranteed to run into the wee hours. Be sure to serve your guests plenty of snacks along with the drinks, or have a late-night supper. One of the best New Year's Eve parties we have attended offered a buffet breakfast soon after midnight. It was a nice way to begin the New Year and sober up the guests at the same time. And, after all, it was morning.

Dress up your party by making it a "Black and White Ball." Ask your guests to wear only black and white, but to be creative in how they apply it. Where one might come in a tux, another might wear a black and white bathing suit. Keep your party color scheme to match.

Or have a regal costume ball, with outlandish getups and flamboyant masks. Award prizes for a variety of costume categories, or vote on the most creative homemade mask.

Since it's New Year's, the beginning of another year, have your guests come seasonally dressed. If you have a good crowd, assign each person or couple a particular month and ask them to dress appropriately. If it's a small group, just assign one of the four seasons. You'll find an appropriate game for this party on page 89.

Another idea is to have a "Highlights of 19XX" party. Ask each guest to come dressed in an outfit that represents a major or minor event that took place during the year. Half the fun is guessing what event each guest represents.

New Year's is also the perfect time for a pajama party. Have your guests wear pajamas and nightgowns for your evening of celebration, and ask them to bring along sleeping bags if you don't have accommodations for all. This way no one has to drive home. Have a pillow fight or ask your guests to "model" their outfits for the crowd while you commentate. In the morning serve a simple breakfast of pastries, juice, and coffee, and maybe some Bloody Marys to perk up the guests.

If you're having the gang over for New Year's Day, center the theme on football and food. Serve a buffet brunch or potluck lunch, and decorate with the team colors. Then sit back and enjoy the game.

And remember to start your planning early so you can enjoy the holidays, too.

INVITATIONS

Begin your New Year celebration with some festive invitations.

● Write your party details on a white card and fill the envelope with colorful confetti. You can make your own by cutting up colored paper, or buy the fancy metallic confetti at gift and card shops.

- Write your party information on a party hat or horn and slip into a large envelope.
- Buy plastic champagne glasses and write details with a felt-tip pen. Tie colorful ribbon to the stem and curl the ends. Hand-deliver or place in box and mail. (Some of the party and cake decorating stores have miniature champagne glasses you might want to use.)
- Take the appropriate page from your new wall or desk calendar (December 31 or Janury 1) and fill in the details on the appropriate square. Photocopy and mail to guests.
- Write your party information on streamers and place them in an envelope.
- Make small clocks from white tagboard and attach black tagboard hands with a fastener. Write party details on the clock.
- Create your own end-of-the-year newspaper by cutting and pasting a current newspaper. Use your typewriter or computer to change the date and to write the party information. Cut and paste into newspaper, photocopy, and mail to guests. Add a few headlines from the past year to enhance it.
- Collect plastic champagne corks from the next wedding you attend (or collect them from your own supply) and write party details with a fine-tip felt pen on the cork, or write details on a card and tie card to cork. Mail in padded envelope.
- For your black-and-white ball, write invitation on white card with black ink, and glue onto slightly larger black card. Ask guests to wear black and white but to be creative in how they apply it. Punch hole in corner and tie with black and white ribbon. Mail in black or white envelope.
- If you're hosting a costume ball, write your party details on an inexpensive mask. You might also ask your guests to turn the mask into a wild false face and wear it to the ball. Tell them there will be prizes for the best one.
- For the overnighter, write your party details on inexpensive toothbrushes, or make teddy bears from con-

struction paper and send them out as invitations. Or draw a moon on the cover and a sun inside to use as a background for your party information.

• If you're having a football party on New Year's Day, write your party details on the favored team's colors. You might ask your guests to dress in the team's colors, too. Or have the men wear old football jerseys and the women dress as cheerleaders, for a hysterical and nostalgic trip back to high school.

DECORATIONS

Decorations for New Year's are usually plentiful and colorful. Here are a few suggestions:

• Spread confetti and streamers all over the party tables. Hang thin paper streamers from the ceiling and tack up wider crepe paper streamers from the center of the room to the walls.

• Fill deflated balloons with a large spoonful of confetti by inserting a funnel into the mouth of the balloon and sliding the confetti inside. Take the balloons to a party shop and ask them to fill them with helium, being careful not to spill the confetti. Tie with colorful ribbon streamers and fill the ceiling with your helium balloons. At midnight, pull down a balloon, hold it over a friend's head, and pop it. . . .

• Make a large tagboard clock with black movable hands. Or make lots of little clocks from the white tagboard. Count down to midnight using the hands of the clock.

• Set your table with white paper plates. Write clock faces on plates in black felt pen and cover with clear Contact.

• Decorate the walls with old newspaper headlines from the past year, or use them as place mats. Paste in a phony headline about each guest to mark his or her place using decorative lettering or your computer.

● If you're hosting the black-and-white ball, keep all your party accessories black and white—tablecloth, place mats, plates, and cups. Blow up black and white balloons, trim with black and white streamers, and make black and white confetti.

● If it's to be a costume party, borrow some costume props from a costume store and use them as a centerpiece and as decorations throughout the house. You can usually find some terrific masks and other items that rent for very little and that really set the mood for your party.

● For your overnighter, hang stars and moons from the ceiling, get out your spare teddy bears for a centerpiece, and play lullaby music during the evening.

● If football is the theme, make pennants for both teams and tack them to the walls. Set your table in the football colors and buy accessories at a sports store—little helmets, football cards, stickers, posters, and so on.

● Make sure you have plenty of horns, hats, and confetti on hand.

GAMES/ACTIVITIES

Here are a few game ideas to help you bring in the new year.

● Every year the newspapers and magazines (*People, Newsweek,* etc.) list the top ten men and women of the year. Save the list and ask your guests to write down who they think are the top ten men and women of the year. Read the answers and award a prize.

● Pick out twelve major events that happened over the year, one from each month. (Check your library for old newspapers or magazines with the year in review.) Mix up the events, read them out loud one at a time, and ask your guests to write down the month that each one took place.

• Here's a variation on that game. Write down some of the more obscure holidays during the year—Groundhog Day, Mother-in-Law Day, National Secretary's Week, National Ice Cream Day—and ask your guests to write the corresponding dates.

• Here's a game that will get everyone laughing. Ask your guests to write three New Year's resolutions. Collect the papers and ask them to listen as you read one of the papers, and guess which guest wrote it.

• Have your guests write predictions for each guest at the party. They can be serious—"Joanne Dahlin will get pregnant," "Len Swec will make his first million,"—or ridiculous—"Bill Simpson will win the lottery," "Melanie Theile will join a nunnery." Read the predictions aloud, then save them and read them again at your next New Year's Party.

• A variation—you write the predictions, but make them general with no names attached. Hide them around the room, attached to an appropriate gift that has been wrapped. For example, if you wrote "You're soon to have another child," attach it to a baby book or bottle of phony birth control pills. Guests are told that some predictions are hidden around the room and as they stumble on one, they are to retrieve it, read the prediction, and open the gift. They are to retrieve only one gift each. It should provide some laughs.

• Ask your guests to come dressed as their favorite year, then have everyone guess the year. Or have them dress as an event that happened during the year.

• Write down some of the major events of the year and ask two guests at a time to act out the scene for everyone to guess.

• Have a White Elephant exchange. Ask each guest to select the worst, ugliest, or most useless present they received for Christmas, or if they didn't get anything really bad, then just something bizarre they've kept hidden away in a dark closet or attic and really don't want. Ask them to wrap the "gifts" beautifully, bring them to the party, and set them under the Christmas tree. According to their birth dates, have the oldest person pick a gift from under the tree and unwrap it for all to admire. The second person then has a choice—he or she can either select a wrapped gift under the tree *or* take away the gift that has just been unwrapped and let the other person select another wrapped gift. Proceed until all guests have opened a present.

• Have a pajama exchange if you're hosting an overnighter. Ask the couples to switch their nightwear and have a parade.

• If you're having a black-and-white ball, ask your guests to make a list of all phrases that have to do with black or white, or both. For example, they might write "We're finally in the black," "She turned white as a ghost," "Nothing's black or white." Have the guest with the longest list read it aloud. Then have other guests read any that were missed, and award a black-and-white gift to the one with the most answers.

• If you're hosting a football party, make a football pool like the one on page 121.

• End the evening with dancing to the year's favorite hits—or have a name-that-tune game using the year's biggest hits, by playing a portion of a song and allowing your guests to race for the title, the artist, and the month it was released.

REFRESHMENTS

Here are a few suggestions for some fancy-to-serve but easy-to-make refreshments.

• Serve champagne with a bright red cherry at the bottom. Or make colorful strawberry or banana daiquiris and serve them with a skewer filled with fruit slices.

• Serve a crème brulée, a rich, elegant dessert that's not difficult to make and requires few ingredients.

In a large saucepan, heat 1 quart heavy cream until bubbles begin to form. *Do not boil.* Add 6 tablespoons sugar and stir until dissolved. Beat 8 egg yolks until lemon-colored. Slowly add hot cream to eggs, stirring constantly until smooth. Add 2 teaspoons vanilla, blend, and pour into 8 custard cups. Place in pan filled with 1 inch hot water and bake 35 minutes at 350°F. Cool and chill 4 hours. Sprinkle 1 cup brown sugar over tops of custards to ¼ inch thick and broil 3 minutes, until sugar has caramelized. *Watch carefully to avoid burning.* Serve well chilled.

● Fill cream puffs with vanilla ice cream and frozen thawed strawberries or fill with chocolate mousse. Top with whipped cream and a cherry.

● If you're serving an after-midnight breakfast, mix up omelet batter and make individual omelets for your guests. Prepare bowls of sliced mushrooms, bacon, ham, green onions, Cheddar cheese, jack cheese, tomatoes, olives, or anything else you like in an omelet. Pour omelet batter in small frying pan and add requested extras. Serve with pour-on cheese sauce or salsa and muffins.

● Eggs Benedict in the morning can be easy if you take a few shortcuts. Just toast English muffins, top them with a slice of Canadian bacon, two soft-boiled or poached eggs, and a homemade cheese sauce or the kind you can buy at the grocery store.

● Make your favorite popover recipe, adding ½ cup grated Cheddar cheese to batter *or* ¼ cup cinnamon. Serve with honey, butter, or jam.

● For your black-and-white ball, serve white chocolate mousse with dark chocolate curls on top. Serve piña coladas and chocolate-coffee.

● The football party works well with a three-foot sandwich (see page 66) or make it "a day at the ballpark" with franks, sauerkraut, hot pretzels, roasted peanuts, and beer.

PRIZES/GIFTS/FAVORS

You might buy a nice wall or desk calendar for the prize winners and send the rest of your guests home with a bottle of champagne, some Alka-Seltzer, or some Bloody Mary mix.

Or how about a copy of *People* or *Newsweek* with the year in review, tied up with a ribbon? Or a copy of a book of predictions?

The black-and-white ball guests could go home with a Polaroid picture of themselves (maybe in black and white) or a black or white mug full of instant black coffee crystals and two white aspirin tablets.

The football fans might be given some of the little sports items you purchased at the athletic store and used as decorations.

OTHER HOLIDAYS

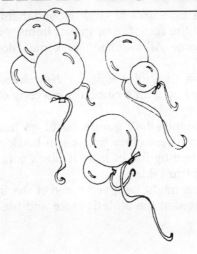

Nearly every month provides us with a major holiday we can celebrate. And according to *Chase's Annual Events*, by William and Mary Chase (Contemporary Books, Chicago, IL: published annually) there are lots of little holidays we can celebrate, too. If you need a theme for your next party, check out *Chase's Annual Events* at your local library and pick a day with an interesting event. You might want to celebrate May Day with a garden party, Arthur Conan Doyle's birthday with a Murder Mystery Party, Millard Fillmore's birthday for no reason at all.

We selected four of the largest holidays to celebrate in this chapter—the four we think make terrific themes for parties.

Valentine's Day parties should be romantic, from the invitations that welcome the guests to the favors you send home at the end of the party. You might want a hearts-and-flowers brunch, or make it a simply elegant dessert. The

Wedding Shower and Anniversary Party might be helpful for additional ideas.

St. Patrick's Day is a great time for a traditional Irish feast. Welcome the Irish and non-Irish alike to help you celebrate this lucky time of year.

The Independence Day picnic is a tradition in our family, and every year it seems to get bigger and better. We've got tips on putting together a picnic, barbecue, luau, or potluck party at the pool, beach, or out by the backyard sprinklers.

And no party book would be complete without a come-as-you-aren't Halloween party. If you've ever wanted to be Romeo in the school play or wondered how you'd look in a Bunny suit, now's your chance. Our haunted Halloween party gives you and your friends a chance to return to childhood and live out a fantasy for a few hours.

And there are plenty of other special days you might want to celebrate—Chinese New Year, Jewish New Year, Easter, Cinco de Mayo, Memorial or Labor Day, Columbus Day, Election Day, or Octoberfest. Nearly any day there's a good excuse for a party!

INVITATIONS

Valentine's Day

• Invite your guests to a Valentine's Day party with lacy heart invitations. Cut out heart shapes from red "velveteen" paper available at the hobby store. Glue onto stiff white tagboard cut a little larger than the red heart. Glue lace trim on the back to form outline around heart and glue on another sheet of white tag to cover edges of lace trim. Write party details on the back and mail to guests.

• Buy small heart-shaped boxes of candy and write party details on white heart-shaped card. Cut to fit inside box, seal, and hand-deliver to guests.

● Buy some little candy hearts that have words on them ("Kiss Me," "I'm Yours"). Write invitation on red heart-shaped tagboard with white ink. Place in envelope. Drop in little candies, or glue them onto the card. Mail to guests.

● Hand-deliver a red rose or red carnation to each of your guests, with a small tag attached with party details.

● Ask guests to dress romantically, or in a red and white theme.

● Ask your guests to come as a favorite romantic hero or heroine.

St. Patrick's Day

● Cut out green clovers from tagboard and green foil wrap. Glue wrap onto tagboard and add party information with green felt-tip pen. Mail in green envelope.

● Buy a lottery ticket for each guest and write party details on a clover-shaped green card. Attach ticket to card with paper clip and mail to guests.

● Some of the stationery stores have small, inexpensive pins with a St. Patrick's Day theme. Attach one to each green invitation and mail.

● Cut out brown construction paper like a large potato,

add a few "eyes" with black felt pen, and write party details on the back.

- Buy a large bag of chocolate gold doubloons. Write party details on fronts and backs of four or five coins and mail in padded envelope.
- Buy some lucky charms—rabbit's foot, medallions, and so on—and attach a card with party invitation. Place in padded envelope and mail.
- Ask your guests to wear as much green as possible.

Independence Day

- Cut out firecracker shapes from red tagboard. Glue glitter at the tip and glue colored ribbon at the end to make streamers. Write details on cone of firecracker. Place in envelope and sprinkle extra glitter inside. Mail to guests.
- Make "poppers" by writing party details on small cards, stuffing them inside paper tubes, and wrapping them with crepe paper. Tie off ends with ribbon and fringe with scissors. Mail in cardboard tube or hand-deliver.

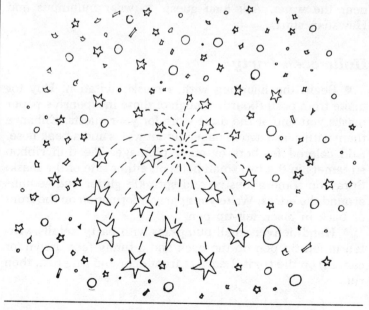

- Buy inexpensive American flags at the party store and write party details on flags. Mail in envelope.
- Write party information on postcards with pictures of the South Seas (or other body of water) for your luau and mail to guests. Or get some Hawaii brochures at the travel agency and write your party information in the margins. Or send them a plastic lei available from the party store, with party details attached.
- Mail paper lunch bags, preferably white, with party details written on the bag. Ask each guest to decorate the bag and fill it with some favorite munchy to bring along to the party.
- Mail invitation in a large envelope with gummed stars stuck all over. Fill the envelope with stars so they tumble out when opened. Make your invitation on a piece of white paper cut out like a star with "Spend the Night Under the Stars" written on the front. Enclose an RSVP card that allows them to check either "Not in the Stars" or "The Stars Will Be Out." Ask all your guests to wear white only.
- Ask guests to bring bathing suits and towels if you'll be near the water. Ask luau guests to wear muumuus and Hawaiian shirts.

Halloween Party

- Begin the haunting with a mask invitation. Buy (or make from posterboard) enough of those inexpensive paper masks you find at the dime store for your guests. Enhance them with construction paper cutout wings and a beak nose. Add colored feathers or other plumage. Tie thin ribbon streamers in the two small holes on either side of the mask. Spray on some adhesive and sprinkle glitter and sequins around the edges. Write your party information on the front or back in black felt-tip pen.
- Hand-deliver small pumpkins with party details written in felt-tip pen on the back and a funny face drawn (or carved) on the front. Leave at front door and ring bell, then run.

- Mail a pumpkin-shaped orange card as party invitation. Fill envelope with candy corn or pumpkin seeds.
- Mail a package of pumpkin seeds with party details written in the margins or glued to the back.
- Design a newspaper ad or poster for a horror movie, with your party details woven into the ad, something like the ads for the movie *Halloween*. Photocopy and mail to guests.
- Ask your guests to come in costume. You can make it a free-for-all, where everyone chooses whatever he or she wants to wear, or make it specific, such as:
  - Dress in fifties (sixties, forties) outfits.
  - Come as your favorite monster.
  - Dress in pairs (so that both the man and woman go together in some way).
  - Come as your mentor.
  - Come as your favorite movie (either just one character from the movie, or odds and ends from the movie made into a unique costume).
  - Come as your favorite singer (then have a lip-sync contest).
  - Come as a cartoon character.
  - Come dressed as if you were eighty years old.
  - Come dressed as a child.
  - Come dressed as your partner's occupation.
  - Come dressed as your hobby.

DECORATIONS

Atmosphere is everything when you give a holiday party. Here are some ways you can set the stage for your production.

Valentine's Day

- Dress the party room in pink, white, and red crepe paper streamers. Or keep it to a red-and-white theme only, with accesories to match.
- Light lots of candles and set them around the room.
- Decorate the center of the room with a bunch of pink, white, and red balloons, or tie one heart-shaped Mylar balloon to the backs of two chairs, joining them together by two ribbons.
- Make up cookie bouquets by baking sugar cookies in heart shapes and pressing wire stems like those used for flower arranging into the backs of the cookies. Decorate the hearts with red, white, and pink icing, gather them carefully together with ribbons, and set them at each place setting. Or place several bouquets in a vase in the center of the table, all tied up with ribbons.
- Put photos of famous romantic couples at each place setting. Hang posters on the walls from romantic movie scenes.
- Play romantic mood music.
- Place roses at each woman's place setting. Or provide them with corsages when they arrive.
- Cut out red and pink paper hearts and hang them from the ceiling or tape them to the walls.
- Make a large paper or felt heart for a place mat.
- Make simple napkins from heart fabric or use red bandannas.
- Set bouquets of flowers on the tables.
- Give all the guys a length of red ribbon and ask them to tie up their lover's hair in a creative way.

- See Wedding Shower and Anniversary Party decorations for more romantic ideas.

St. Patrick's Day

- Cut out large green clovers and tack them to the walls.
- Cut out a large tree from brown and green tagboard and attach to one wall. Set the party food near the tree. Buy a "rainbow" at a party or novelty store and hang it on the wall, making sure one end lands at the tree, right at the food—the "pot of gold."
- Make a treasure chest from a shirt box wrapped with gold wrapping paper. Fill the box with chocolate coins and leave partly open.
- Decorate with lucky charms—horseshoes, rabbit's feet, medallions, "blarney" stones, four-leaf clovers, and so on.
- Accent with anything green—green sprayed daises, green candles, bowls of green jelly beans, and so on.
- Make large shamrocks from construction paper or felt for place mats. Serve drinks in beer mugs, whether it's beer or not. (If it's beer, tint it green.)
- Make an unusual centerpiece using potatoes. Cut out small paper shamrocks, tape them to toothpicks, and stick them into the potatoes. Fill the cracks between the potatoes with gold candy coins.
- Set a large smooth rock in the center of the table. Thickly color your lips with red lipstick and make kiss marks all over the "blarney" stone.
- Get some posters of Ireland from the poster store or some brochures from the travel agency and place them along the walls.

Independence Day

- Set out small American flags stuck into hunks of white cheese or dip.
- Hang red, white, and blue crepe paper streamers from

the ceiling. Decorate the patio or backyard with white or colored Christmas lights.

• Serve food in beach pails or terra cotta flower pots. Fill a wheelbarrow with ice and cold drinks.

• Get out all your beach paraphernalia and ask your guests to bring along anything they might have that would be appropriate at the beach, pool, and so on.

• Use red or blue bandannas for place mats or napkins, or buy inexpensive straw fans to, use as place mats. Tie napkin to handle of fan, and use for cooling off when it's hot.

• Make extra tables for large crowds by resting a large board on two saw horses and cover with a red, white, or blue tablecloth.

• Cover tables with red-checked tablecloths or buy inexpensive fabric in red, white, and blue and make your own cloths. Use two colors and two sizes of paper plates, one on top of the other.

• Spread large towels or old sheets and blankets over grass or dirt for picnicking.

• Hire a school or other band to play music.

• Play a John Philip Sousa marching tape for background music to get things started.

• Control bugs with bug lights or bug zappers, and spray yard with bug repellent an hour before party.

• For luau, float candles or gardenias or other flowers in the pool. Play Hawaiian music. Decorate fence with torches, large fishnets, travel posters of Hawaii, big fish.

Halloween

• You can purchase small bags of "cobwebs" or make your own from fiberfill. Carefully pull apart the fiberfill to create webs and stick them to any rough wall or ceiling surface, or tape the ends with small pieces of Scotch tape. The webs look best when framing the front door, or windows, but can be stretched from a light fixture to a wall or table, too.

• Place several rubber spiders or other rubber creepy

crawlers in the webs, and hang the rest from the ceiling using black thread and Scotch tape.

- But several small votive candles and inexpensive holders to go with them. Place them all around the party room. Add a few tapered candles, too.
- Pick up a couple of records or tapes from horror movie soundtracks—*Rocky Horror Picture Show, Phantom of the Opera,* whatever is available. If you have a video player, rent a couple of horror movies—*Night of the Living Dead, Halloween, Young Frankenstein*—and play them in the background.
- Carve some pumpkins and turn them into hideous jack-o'-lanterns. Try to be creative and make them as ugly as possible. Maybe you could give them names of guests and use them as place cards.
- Hang orange and black crepe paper streamers in doorways, from top of opening to floor so guests have to brush them aside to get in.
- Have a "ghost" greet the guests as they enter by blowing up a large balloon, then tying it off with black string. Cut a tiny hole in the center of an old sheet and slip the string through. Let the sheet fall over the balloon, to form ghost. Draw two black circles for eyes and hang the ghost with the black string from the ceiling in the center of the room.
- To greet your guests, and discourage unwanted spirits, place two chairs on the front porch. Stuff two sets of old clothes, one man and one woman, and set them up in the chairs to look like real bodies. Find a couple of tall tables, short ladders, or boxes you can stack, and put them behind the chairs. Set two jack-o'-lanterns on top, just at the point where the heads should be, to make your bodies "come alive." For added fun, set one of the heads in one of the body's arms to make a "headless" host.
- Play scary Halloween records in the background, available at record stores.
- Make your centerpiece mini-jack-o'-lanterns. Cut the tops off oranges as you would a pumpkin. Scoop out insides,

and place a votive candle inside. Draw funny jack-o'-lantern faces on oranges with felt-tip pen. Sprinkle some gummy worms and spiders around the table.

GAMES/ACTIVITIES

Valentine's Day

● Most of the games suggested for the Wedding Shower and Anniversary Party will be appropriate for your Valentine's Party, so refer back to pages 13 and 52 for ideas.

● Love coupons are a lot of fun at a romantic Valentine's Party. On red paper hearts, write up one "love coupon" per guest, good for some activity or special treat that would appeal to couples in love. You might include such tokens as: "Good for one long kiss on demand," "Good for one massage," "Good for one dinner at a favorite restaurant," "Good for a foot rub," "Good for time off from a least-favorite chore." Make at least three of the coupons duds, like: "Good for one headache at the appropriate time," "Good for one mandatory call to mother-in-law," "Good for hearing and correcting one major fault." Fold the coupons in half, mix them up, and place them in a heart-shaped box. Explain that each guest gets a love coupon and that they are to oblige the request on demand from their partner at any time. Have them read their chosen coupons aloud to the group.

● Go around to each couple and have them tell how they met.

● Go around to each couple and have them tell about their first date.

● Go around to each couple and ask where was the "first time."

● Go around to each guest and ask what was (or is) attractive about partner.

• Play "Write a Romance." Go around from guest to guest and create your own "romance." Ask the first guest to start the story with a lusty beginning. After a few moments, stop and go to the next guest. Ask that person to embellish on the story. Continue from guest to guest until all have added to the story and it is brought to a conclusion.

• Play a variation on the above game by having each guest write down the worst opening line to a romance he or she can come up with. Have them all read their openers.

• Play "Love Slogans." Have each player take a turn giving a love slogan, such as "Love is blind," "I love my St. Bernard," or "Love stinks." One by one have them drop out if they can't come up with a slogan until you're down to the winner.

St. Patrick's Day

• Give guests lottery tickets and have them scratch the tickets one by one.

• Hide the lottery tickets (or other lucky charms) throughout the house and let guests search for them. Tell them they can have only one per person.

• Have everyone write down as many superstitions as they can think of, such as "Don't let a black cat cross your path," or "A broken mirror brings seven years bad luck." Read them aloud, and give a prize to the lucky winner who has the most.

• One at a time, have everyone name something Irish. Keep going until only one person is able to name anything more.

• Use an almanac to find some facts about Ireland. List them, along with some bogus ones, and read the list aloud, asking your guests to note which ones are true and which are false. Award a prize for the most correct answers.

• Read the following list of names and ask which ones were born in Ireland: Roger Moore, Roddy McDowall, Rod McKuen, Patrick McGoohan, Ed McMahon, Edmund O'Brien, Carroll O'Connor, Sean Connery. (The answer is none: London, London, Oakland, Queens, Detroit, Milwaukee, New York City, Scotland.)

Independence Day

- Check the Family Reunion (page 64) for ideas on outdoor games.
- Give everyone—kids and adults—a squirt gun and have a water war.
- Get out the old favorites—volleyball, croquet, horseshoes, lawn darts—and set them around the area for your guests.
- Have groups enact some event from American history for all to guess.
- Make up box lunches as for the Family Reunion and have each guest bid something creative and funny for the lunch he or she wants.
- Name several dates in history and quiz the group on what happened.
- Have guests tell what they like about America and what they might change.
- Have each person tell about some unusual and out-of-the-way place in America he or she has visited.
- If you're having a luau, do the limbo and have a best Hawaiian costume award.
- Another idea for the luau—have the men make their own grass skirts from large paper bags, crepe paper, or other paper. Then have them all do their version of the hula.

Halloween

- Gather the ghouls together for a costume-judging contest. You might want to award a prize just for "Best Costume," or turn it into a main event with "Ugliest Costume," "Most Embarrassing Costume," "Most Original Costume," "Costume With the Most Work Spent On It," "Costume That Took the Most Nerve to Wear," and so on.

106

• You've heard of bobbing for apples? How about bobbing for olives in a martini! Fill enough plastic champagne or wide-mouthed beverage glasses for all guests with 1 jigger vermouth and 3 jiggers gin or vodka. Drop 5 olives in each glass. Line the glasses around a table so that each guest has access to a glass. On the count of three, with hands behind backs, each guest is to bob into the martini and try to collect all five olives in his mouth at the same time using only his *tongue*. Whoever collects them first must raise a hand (he or she certainly won't be able to yell "I won!").

• Tell your guests it's time to play "Pass the Donut." Collect toothpicks and cut off the very sharp tips on each end, with scissors. Divide the group into two teams and line them up. Hand each person a toothpick and ask them to place it in their mouths and put their hands behind their backs. Tell your guests you couldn't find a donut anywhere around the house, so you're using a Cheerio instead. On the count of three, stick a Cheerio on the first teammate's toothpick and have them pass it on to the next player's toothpick. If it drops, whoever dropped it must pick it up and return it to his own toothpick. The team that passes it to the last player first, wins.

• Play "Creepy Quotes." Distribute paper and pencil and have your guests number from 1 to 10. Read aloud the following quotes from famous horror movies and ask the guests to name the film. Award a point for each right answer—the most points wins.

1. "It's alive!" *(Frankenstein)*
2. "Even a man who is pure in heart and says his prayers at night . . . may become a wolf when the wolfbane blooms and the moon is full and bright." *(The Wolfman)*
3. "Slowly I turned, step by step, inch by inch, and then I grabbed him . . ." *(Abbott and Costello Meet Frankenstein)*
4. "It's not Frankenstein, it's Frankensteen. It's not Eegor, it's Eyegor." *(Young Frankenstein)*
5. "Three more days till Halloween." *(Halloween, Part II)*

6. "You'll just be staying the one night?" *(Psycho)*
7. "They're here . . ." *(Poltergeist).*
8. "Heeerrre's Johnny!" *(The Shining)*
9. "Stay on the path. Keep away from the moors." *(American Werewolf in London)*
10. "Is there someone inside you?" *(The Exorcist)*
11. "Make no mistake—this is not a human child." *(The Omen)*
12. "Wake up! They get you when you sleep. They grow out of those pods." *(Invasion of the Body Snatchers)*
13. "What have you done to its eyes?" *(Rosemary's Baby)*
14. "Michael! Did you hear your father? Out of the water—*now!*" *(Jaws)*
15. "You wouldn't be able to do these awful things to me if I weren't in this chair." "Oh, but you *are*, Blanche. You are!" *(Whatever Happened to Baby Jane?)*

• Have a lip-sync contest if your guests are dressed in fifties' or sixties' costume. Play records from those years and have each person do his number.

• Have a pumpkin-carving contest. Give each guest or couple a pumpkin and ask them to carve it creatively. The best, worst, ugliest, and so on win prizes.

• Have each guest act out a horrible scene from a horror movie. You might write some titles on slips of paper to get them started, such as *Psycho, Halloween, Jaws, Nightmare on Elm Street, Frankenstein, The Bride,* and so on. This is fun, easy, and perfect for Halloween.

REFRESHMENTS

Here's a wide range of refreshments to serve your celebrating guests, from easy-but-elegant desserts to plentiful picnic fare.

Valentine's Day

• If you're having a brunch, serve mimosas (champagne mixed with orange juice) with a strawberry at the bottom of the glass.

• Quiches are easy, make-ahead brunch dishes that please nearly everyone.

• Make a pink salmon mousse in a heart shape.

• Serve the cookie bouquets as dessert (see page 100), or make a giant chocolate chip cookie and use it first as a centerpiece and then as a refreshment.

• If you're having a dessert, serve croissants filled with fresh strawberries or canned cherry-pie filling. Top with chocolate sauce and whipped cream.

• Also for dessert, cut small cantaloupes in half and remove seeds. Cut out melon flesh and save, and cut a small slice at the bottom of each melon half so it will stand without wobbling. Fill melon opening with cantaloupe mixed with raspberries, blueberries, and strawberries. Or fill a large melon with a mixture of ¼ cup yogurt, ¼ cup honey, ¼ cup coconut, and 16 ounces cottage cheese. Assemble sliced fruit around melon for dipping.

• Fill crepes with pecan ice cream and top with melted chocolate sauce.

• Serve crab sandwiches on sliced French bread, with Cheddar cheese slices, bacon, and shredded lettuce.

St. Patrick's Day

• Serve some of the traditional Irish dishes at your St. Patrick's Day dinner—corned beef and cabbage, potatoes, Irish stew.

• Offer your guests a do-it-yourself stuffed potato. Line up bowls of 'tater toppings—crumbled bacon, diced ham, shredded cheese, chopped cooked broccoli, cooked peas, sour cream, butter, and so on—and let your guests fill their hot baked potatoes.

• Serve potato skins. Bake potatoes, cut in half, and

scoop out meat. Deep-fry skins until crisp and fill with shredded Cheddar cheese, green onion, crumbled bacon, and serve with ranch dressing.

• Make or buy large pretzels and hang them around the necks of the guests so they can munch on them while drinking their beer.

• Wash everything down with green beer. There are a couple of green beers on the market, or tint your own keg with food coloring.

Independence Day

• A potluck is the easiest way to handle large crowds. Read the chapter on Family Reunions (page 57) for ideas on how to organize a potluck picnic.

• If you're barbecuing, jazz up those plain old hamburgers and hot dogs. Grill the burgers and dogs to order, then let your guests choose from a large array of toppings to create their own bodacious burgers and humungous hot dogs. Some suggestions for toppings: guacamole, pesto sauce, salsa, sour cream, chutney, melted jalapeño cheese, shredded cheeses, sautéed mushrooms, sautéed onions and garlic, green and red pepper slices, tomato slices, strips of bacon, pickles and relish, and your special secret sauce— catsup, mayonnaise, and mustard mixed together.

• Here's a different way to serve burgers and beans. Place hamburger patties in large muffin tins, individual casserole dishes, or custard cups, and shape to fit. Bake at 350°F for 10 minutes. Turn onto paper towels to absorb grease. Set upright on plates and top with warm baked beans.

• If you're in charge of salads, here's an easy, eye-catching one that's guaranteed to please. And for convenience, you make it a day ahead. In a large glass salad bowl, layer shredded lettuce, 1 can sliced water chestnuts, 2½ cups shredded cooked chicken, 1 cup chopped celery, ½ cup chopped green pepper, ½ cup chopped red onion, ½ cup mushrooms, and 1 package uncooked frozen peas. Spread 1

pint mayonnaise over the top of the salad to seal. Cover and refrigerate 8 hours. Before serving, add 6 ounces grated Cheddar cheese and 10 slices crumbled cooked bacon.

• For dessert, scoop out one half of a watermelon (save or eat the watermelon). Fill shell with raspberry sherbet and smooth to form "watermelon." Stick chocolate chips in two rows along each side to make "seeds." Keep frozen until serving time.

• Carve your watermelon with a fancy design, then fill with mixed fruit or use it as a punch bowl and fill with cranberry punch.

• Serve an elegant dessert that's easy to make. Dip fresh strawberries in melted white chocolate and skewer on Styrofoam cone to make "tree."

• For your luau, serve your guests piña coladas in hollowed-out coconuts with a straw. Saw the coconut in half or saw off the top part to create a container.

- Set a bottle of juice in a milk carton and set four flowers between the juice and the carton. Fill carton with water and freeze. At picnic time, tear off carton to reveal flowers set in ice. Serve ice cold juice.
- Cut a pineapple in half and cut flesh into chunks. Mix pineapple with maraschino cherries and replace in pineapple "shell." Serve with marshmallow sauce.
- It's not a summertime picnic or party without homemade ice cream.

Halloween

- There's nothing like a Bloody Mary to give atmosphere to your party.
- Or welcome your guests with a mug of "witches brew." Combine 1 pint cranberry juice cocktail, 1 bottle Burgundy wine, 2 sticks cinnamon, 1 lemon, thinly sliced, 1 cup water, ½ cup sugar, and 6 whole cloves in large pan. Cover and heat on low for 1 to 2 hours. Carve out pumpkin and rinse thoroughly. Pat dry. Draw a hideous face with black felt-tip pen on the outside. When ready to serve punch, pour into cleaned-out pumpkin shell.
- "Frozen pumpkins" make a perfect dessert for the hungry guests. You'll need 1 orange per guest, and a half-gallon vanilla ice cream mixed with 1 8-ounce can pumpkin pie mix to fill 8 to 12 oranges. Clean out oranges (save pulp and juice for breakfast) and pat dry. Draw little jack-o'-lantern faces on oranges in black felt-tip pen. Soften ice cream. When soft, scoop into bowl and stir in can of pumpkin. Blend thoroughly. Scoop ice cream into individual oranges and freeze. Set out 5 minutes before serving.

PRIZES/GIFTS/FAVORS

Valentine's Day

- Box of candy.
- Bouquet of flowers.
- Bouquet of cookies.
- Romance magazine or book.
- Theater tickets or movie passes.
- Bottle or split of champagne.
- Stationery, a mug, or other item that has "lips" on it.
- Poster of a hunk or babe.
- Romantic album.
- Romantic cologne/after shave.
- Massage oil.
- Mylar balloons with a romantic picture and saying.
- Book of poems.

St. Patrick's Day

- Lottery ticket.
- Lucky charms, such as a rabbit's foot.
- Your secret recipe for Irish stew.
- Six-pack of green beer.
- Sack of Irish potatoes or a bag of potato chips.
- Bag of chocolate gold coins.
- Stationery or other item with a rainbow design.
- Irish folk songs.
- Large poster of Ireland.
- Shamrock pins.

Independence Day

- Beach toy.
- Suntan lotion or oil.
- Sunglasses.

- Bandanna.
- Beach towel.
- Rattan beach mat.
- Visor.
- Squirt gun.
- Fourth of July pin.
- Gardenia corsages.
- Plastic or candy lei.
- A guidebook on Hawaii.
- Jar of macadamia nuts.
- Bag of Hawaiian potato chips.
- Hawaiian beer (Primo).

Halloween

- A pair of passes to the local horror movie.
- Pumpkin.
- Mask.
- Creepy record.
- Trick or treat bag filled with gourmet candy.
- Gummy rats and worms.
- Paperback mystery novels.
- Old radio show on tape—the scary ones like *The Shadow*, *Mystery Theater*, or *War of the Worlds*.

PRIVATE SCREENINGS

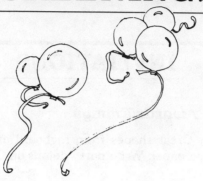

In this day of big-screen television sets, video cassette players, and video stores, it's easy to plan a private screening in your own home.

We've got four themes for private screenings you might want to host for your friends:

Have an "Academy Awards" or "Emmys" night and ask your friends to come dressed in formal gowns and black tie, just as they'd dress for the real Hollywood event. Or have them dress as one of the characters nominated for an award. Serve a sit-down dinner or just cocktails and hors d'oeuvres.

Throw a "Grammys" or "Country Music Awards" dinner dance. Ask your guests to come dressed in fifties or sixties clothes, or dress country-style, with overalls, bandannas, and pigtails.

The Super Bowl and World Series make a great excuse for a party. Use some of the ideas from the New Year's Day party, such as having your guests come in football/cheerleader outfits or in the home team's colors. Make it a buffet lunch with lots of snacks and beer.

Rent a new video or pick out an old classic and have a few friends over for a "Video Night." Keep it simple with light snacks or serve something related to the movie if appropriate—Southern cooking for an evening of *Gone with the Wind* or fish and chips while you watch *Jaws*.

INVITATIONS

Academy Awards/Emmys

● Cut out Oscar shapes from tagboard and cover with gold wrapping paper. Write party details on Oscar and mail to guests.

● If your party will be black tie, cut out a black bow tie from black tagboard and write party information in white ink (or vice versa). Mail to guests.

● Cut out pictures of the nominees from magazines and have them photocopied. Write question marks around them or write in some funny comments. Add party details and mail to friends.

● Cut out oversized theater tickets from tagboard and write party information to resemble real tickets. Mail a pair to your guests.

● Cut out stars from silver paper to use as invitations. Fill the envelope with gummed stars.

● Send ballot forms along with invitation so the guests can fill them out before the party begins. Ask them to bring the ballots to the party.

Grammys/County Music Awards

● Cut out record shapes or musical notes from tagboard and write party information on one side. Mail in large envelopes.

● Buy some photo postcards of your favorite recording

stars at the record store and write party details on the back. Add a stamp and mail.

• Buy some sheet music of nominated songs and write party information along the lines. Photocopy and send to music-loving guests. Or use blank sheet music to write your invitation. Make some of the letters look like musical notes.

• Cut out musical notes from black construction paper and write party details in white ink. Drop in envelope and mail to guests.

• Send ballots.

Super Bowl/World Series

• Cut out footballs or baseballs so they fold and write party information inside. Mail in envelopes.

• Buy some football or baseball cards at the sports or variety stores and write party details on the back. Stick in envelope and mail.

• Photocopy an old sports program sheet and add party information. Mail.

• Photocopy part of the sports page, substituting your party details in one of the columns. Send to party guests.

Video Night

• Cut out something appropriate symbolizing the movie, such as a shower curtain if you're planning to show *Psycho* or a gorilla for *King Kong* and mail to guests.

• Some poster stores have small postcards of old movies you can use for your party invitations.

• Buy a picture of the star of the movie you're showing and mail copies to your guests with party details on the back.

• Buy movie magazines and tear out pictures of stars. Write party details as speech balloons and mail to guests.

• Buy popcorn bags at the party supply house or from a local theater and write party details right on the bag. Fill envelope with a few popcorn kernels.

- Make some oversized theater tickets from tagboard and write name of movie and party details on the ticket.

DECORATIONS

Since the focus at your private screening party is the screen, you can keep the decorations simple. Here are a few things you might want to try:

Academy Awards/Emmys

- Buy posters of movie stars at the poster shop and hang them on the walls near your screen. Use them as prizes if you have games at your party.
- Cut out white tagboard in star shapes and glue glitter on them. Hang from the ceiling in the party room.
- Make a large colorful chart of the nominees, with photos if possible, to score the events during the evening.
- Hang a few movie phrases on the wall, such as "Frankly, Scarlett, I don't give a damn."
- Find items relating to the five nominations for best picture and set them up as a centerpiece for your table.
- Make ballots for voting on the awards and use them as place mats at your table. Set out some trophies and label them "Oscars." Cover the table with star-studded fabric.
- Play music from one of the movie soundtracks until the party begins.
- Decorate the party room with black and silver streamers draped from the ceiling to the walls. It makes a formal-looking and impressive atmosphere for celebrity-viewing.

Grammy/Country Music Awards

- Hang posters of recording artists on the walls.
- Cut out black musical notes to hang from the ceiling.

- Make a chart for recording the winners.
- Set up, build, or rent a wooden dance floor if you don't have floor space in your home. Put up a mirror ball and rent some strobe lights.
- Play albums in the background before or after the party.
- Set out blank sheet music for place mats. Keep the color scheme black and white, with red accents.
- If you're celebrating the country music awards, use checked tablecloths and napkins, and set up a country-looking centerpiece, with brown eggs, wisps of hay, a gingham chicken, and some bandannas.
- Hang some music phrases around the room, such as "Drop-kick me, Jesus, through the goalposts of life."
- If you're watching the Grammys, set the stage with new-wave props, such as colorful jewelry, bright scarves, and record jackets.

Super Bowl/World Series

- Hang posters of the team or star players.
- Hang tagboard footballs or baseballs from ceiling.
- Decorate the party room in the team colors (see page 89).
- Write up a few statistic questions and hang them on the walls. Such things as "Who had the most home runs in the first World Series?"
- You might rent or devise a small set of bleachers to sit on. Or arrange your furniture in a half circle to simulate a stadium.
- Mark out the living room with gridirons and set up a few goalposts.
- Set the table with old game programs as place mats.
- Use a Ping-Pong table as your serving table and tape it with white tape to look like the gridiron.
- Make a centerpiece of footballs, pennants, and peanuts. Or add a touch of whimsy with some Ace bandages, Ben-Gay, and crushed beer cans.

Video Night

- Buy movie posters and put them up in the TV room.
- Hang appropriate items from the ceiling that relate to the movie, such as little spaceships for *Star Wars*.
- Make a centerpiece of appropriate items from the movie.
- Make place mats by tearing out pictures of the stars and covering them with clear Contact.
- Arrange the party room to resemble the movie set for atmosphere. For example, if it's a scary movie, get out a few masks, dim the lights, and use candles.
- Put up some quotes from the movie, such as "Play it, Sam."
- Greet your guests in a costume from the movie.
- Make an eye-catching centerpiece with a huge bowl of popcorn set on some old movie reels. Make place mats from popcorn bags.
- Set up your wet bar to look like a theater candy counter.

GAMES/ACTIVITIES

You won't need too many games for your private screening party since most of the time is taken up watching the screen. But during those commercial interruptions you might want to have a few games ready.

Academy Awards/Emmys

- Have everyone bet who will win in each category. Make up a sheet with all the categories and nominees listed so your guests can circle their guesses before the show begins. Whoever has the most right answers wins a prize.
- Provide rubber-tipped dart guns so the guests can shoot the unpopular winners on the screen.

• Visit the library and look up award winners from the past—there are several books available, one in particular called *Fifty Golden Years of Oscar: The Official History of the Academy of Motion Picture Arts & Sciences,* ($24.95, ESE California, La Habra, CA: 1979). Write down the titles of the movies and best actor/actress winners. Scramble them up on a sheet of paper and ask guests to name the year when they won.

• If you have the Silver Screen Edition of Trivial Pursuit, play an informal game during the commercials, by reading off the questions and racing for the first to answer.

• Write down famous lines from award-winning movies and have your guests guess what movie you're quoting.

• Give each guest or couple a part from the movie and have them act it out for the others to guess.

Grammys/Country Music Awards

• Bet on the winners.
• More rubber-tipped darts for the angry mob.
• Ask questions from the RPM edition of Trivial Pursuit during commercials.
• Write down lines from songs on a sheet of paper and ask your guests to write down the titles and artists.
• Have a dance contest.
• Before the party begins, record just a few seconds of each of your records, allowing about ten seconds of blank tape in between songs. Distribute paper and pencil. Play the tape for your guests, asking them to "Name That Tune." Replay the tape and name the songs, allowing guests to check their answers. The most right answers wins (a record?).

Super Bowl/World Series

• Bet on the winner.
• More rubber-tipped darts for the fans.
• Play the Sports edition of Trivial Pursuit.

- Use your almanac to find information about sports figures. Write questions and hang them on the walls. Ask guests to write down their answers between innings or quarters.

Video Night

- Since there shouldn't be any commercials during your video screening, just enjoy the movie. Take a few notes as you watch, then quiz your guests at the end of the movie.
- Play movie title charades.
- Take turns quoting from movies and having one another guess the movie title.
- Do a little research on the stars of the movie for some video trivia.

REFRESHMENTS

Keep the food simple at your private screening. Munchies to snack on during the show and a dessert at the end is all you really need. Here are a few suggestions for all four parties:

- No private screening is complete without popcorn. Flavor it with spices and seasonings (see page 43) and serve it in popcorn bags that are available from party supply stores.
- Heat a pot of cheese or chocolate fondue. Serve bread and veggies with the cheese; fruit, marshmallows, and nuts with the chocolate.
- Offer your guests a do-it-yourself salad bar. Set out bowls of salad makings and let them help themselves.(Or ask everyone to bring a contribution.)
- Set out a cheese/bread hors d'oeuvre the fans can tear apart as they watch the screen. Buy a large round loaf of French bread and cut halfway into it in a crisscross pattern.

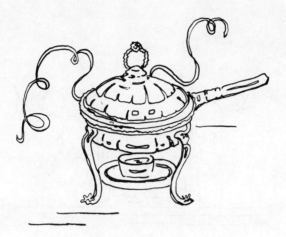

Insert slices of Cheddar cheese in one direction and Monterey Jack cheese in the other direction. Top with melted butter, Parmesan cheese, garlic salt or powder, and black pepper. Broil until cheeses are melted.

● Hot chili and corn bread make a great crowd pleaser. It's simple, filling, and fun.

● Make a veggie dip from mashed avocados and sour cream. Serve carrot sticks, zucchini sticks, celery sticks, green pepper sticks, and cherry tomatoes.

● How about peanuts in the shell, trail mix, bread sticks with cheese dip, or pistachios in the shell for an easy snack offering?

● For dessert, make a pan of brownies and slice into large squares. Top with vanilla ice cream, banana slices, strawberry slices, fudge sauce, whipped cream, and a cherry. Quick, easy, stunning, and delicious!

● Pour champagne for your black tie party, otherwise offer your guests an array of foreign bottled beers to taste and compare.

● For your Super Bowl party, hire some kids to serve the food as vendors, with boxes of goodies tied around their necks.

PRIZES

You won't need gifts or favors at your private screening, but if you play games you may want to pick up some prizes.

For the Academy Awards/Emmys, give the winners movie or theater tickets, posters, or movie magazines.

Recordings of favorite artists would be good gifts for the Grammys/Country Music Awards party, as well as blank tapes, a rock'n'roll T-shirt, or concert tickets.

The sports fans would love tickets to a game for a prize, or maybe a pennant, a sweatshirt with the team logo, or a sports statistics book.

Send the video viewer home with a coupon good for a free video movie, theater tickets, a huge bag of pre-popped popcorn, or a blank video tape.

COMING AND GOING PARTIES

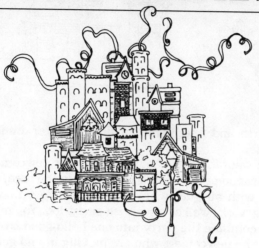

It seems as if so many of our friends have moved away in the past several years, most of them because of job transfers. As I watch them pack those large cartons, hang out the garage sale signs, and return all the little borrowed items they've collected over the years, I hardly feel like celebrating.

But instead of sitting around feeling sorry for myself, wishing I weren't losing another good friend, I plan a going-away-get-together they're unlikely to forget, no matter what their destination.

A "movable feast" or "progressive dinner" is a great way to host a Moving Away party. Ask three other guests if they're willing to host part of the party, then divide the evening into quarters. Begin with drinks and hors d'oeuvres at your place, then move on to the next house for salad/soup. Dine at the third house for the main course, and wrap it up

at a fourth and final home for dessert, after-dinner drinks and coffee.

If you want to have a housewarming for newcomers in the neighborhood or old friends relocating in the area, make it a potluck with all guests bringing a favorite dish. A housewarming works well as a surprise party, too. You might even want to combine the party into one hello-good-bye event—hello to the newcomers who are moving in and good-bye to the old friends who are moving out.

More and more people are traveling these days, and if you have friends who are taking off for their dream vacation to Tahiti, Alaska, or the Himalayas, throw them a surprise Bon Voyage party and serve a typical meal from the destination point.

INVITATIONS

Moving Away

• Begin your party with invitations made from baggage claim tags, available at most airline terminals, or make your own from tagboard and colored paper.

- Reproduce some airline tickets by whiting out information on old ones and filling in your party details, or make your own from tagboard.
- Send for brochures of the destination from the Chamber of Commerce and write your party details inside.
- Include on your invitations information about the movable feast if you're having one, and whether it's a surprise.
- In your invitation, ask your group of friends to bring or mail in memorable photos from past events—the ski weekend, the camping trip, the Amazon River raft ride, or just the yearly Halloween party. Collect the photos into an album, write some funny captions, and present it to the relocating guest during the party. Or ask the guests to bring a photograph of their family to give to the movers.
- Ask each guest to bring the name, address, and phone number (and possibly photo) of someone they know in the mover's new city. The lucky mover will then have several new contacts.
- You might also ask your friends to dress up in caricature a bit, to help the movers feel at home in their new environment. For example, if they're traveling to a new state, like California or Florida, dress stereotypically— Hawaiian shirts, sunglasses, sandals. If the weather's likely to be different from what they're used to, wear raincoats (Oregon), ski outfits (Alaska), or swimsuits (the tropics). With a little imagination, you'll soon have a roomful of Hollywood starlets, Dallas cowboys, or Iowa farmers.

Housewarming

- Have an artist/friend draw a sketch of the new house. Photocopy and fold into a card, write party details inside.
- Cut out a mailbox shape from colored tagboard and write new address on mailbox. Have it open and write party details inside, or make a slit and stick in a small "letter" with party details that can be pulled out.

- For a little fun, find a picture of a tumbledown shack and photocopy it. Write party details on the back.
- Reproduce sections of the map where the new folks are headed to use as invitations.
- Tie up a white card with a yellow ribbon that symbolizes "Welcome Home," write party details on card, and mail to guests.
- Be sure to mention if it's a surprise, and tell the guests where to meet so you can be standing together on the doorstep with your potluck dishes and gifts.

Bon Voyage

- Find some appropriate postcards that symbolize the vacation spot and send them to your guests. For example, if they're headed for the tropics, pick out pictures of beaches. If Disney World is their destination, send out pictures of Mickey Mouse.
- Send little inexpensive items that represent the vacation spot with party details written on a baggage claim ticket and tied onto the item. For example, send a plastic lei if a Hawaiian vacation is planned, or an apple if they're headed for New York.
- Write party details on travel brochures of destination and mail to guests.
- If the guests of honor are headed for a foreign country, write the invitation in that language.
- Again, if it's to be a surprise, mention that in the invitation.
- Ask your guests to dress suitably for the vacation spot. Have them wear kilts for Scotland, safari wear for Kenya, or Mickey Mouse hats for Disneyland. Or just come dressed as tacky tourists.

DECORATIONS

Moving Away

• On a large sheet of tagboard, outline the mover's destination. Get out the atlas and mark down all real or imaginary points of interest. Most states have several funny-sounding towns that can be marked with a gummed star. Tape one end of yarn near star and pull out to wall. On colored paper, write a phony description of the place— "Paris, Texas . . . Not exactly an 'eyeful,' " "Amityville, New York . . . A 'spirited' city," "Naughtright, New Jersey . . . Home of Murphy's Law." Tape description to other end of yarn.

• The caricature dress-ups mentioned in the invitations will also add to the atmosphere. And perhaps you can have some T-shirts made with "New Jersey or Bust," "California Here I Come," or "I (heart) New York." Here's an idea for a T-shirt that was a hit at one of our going-away parties: Most cities and states offer T-shirts with their names emblazoned on the front. If not, have one made up, with the name of the city or state your movers are *leaving*. Then ask the T-shirt makers for one of those red circles with the red line through it—the international sign for "No." (Some places sell these plain, others have something already crossed out. Ask the clerk to cut off everything but the red circle and line.) Have them place it on top of your home town or state and press it on. Then, underneath, place the letters of the destination— not too neat—and press that on. They'll get a lot of curious looks and questions when they walk down the street in this T-shirt!

• If there are some items that are famous for the new territory, place them together to make a centerpiece. For example, a ten-gallon hat for Texas, a variety of cheese for Wisconsin, a bowlful of pasta for Italy. Think about the joke gifts, too—a rubber worm in an apple for New York. . . .

• Make place settings from the state or country flags and use the state or country colors for your color scheme.
• If the destination suggests any particular music, play it in the background during the party. For example, if they're headed for New York, play "New York, New York." If Tennessee will soon be home, keep the country music flowing.

Housewarming

• If the people are new in the area, a map on the wall with useful points of interest would be decorative and helpful—the best market, the cheapest gas station, the most popular restaurant. If they're just relocating locally, you can use the map with funny spots of interest—use your imagination.
• If they're new, buy samples from various stores and use them as a centerpiece and gift at the same time. Things like croissants from your favorite bakery, a knickknack from a gift shop, and so on.
• Tie up props in the party room with yellow ribbons of welcome.
• Photocopy sections of the local map to use as place mats.

Bon Voyage

• A map of the vacation area would be handy and colorful.
• Hang posters and pictures depicting the vacation spot.
• Arrange items from the area as a centerpiece—pineapples and fishnets from Hawaii; teapot, teas, and cakes for England; happy faces and suntan lotion for California.
• Set up the party room as an airplane, cruise ship, or scene from the destination. Greet the guests in flight-crew uniforms (borrowed, rented, or makeshift) and play music or a video from an airplane movie or the destination. Have part of the party "in flight" and part "on arrival."

GAMES/ACTIVITIES

Games are always fun at Coming and Going Parties. Here are a few suggestions that will work for Moving Away, Housewarming, and Bon Voyage parties with a few adaptations.

Guided Tour

Sometime before the party, run around your local town and take slide shots of some of the "highlights." Prepare your slides into a travelog by reviewing the pictures and jotting down a note or two about each site. The twist is, as you show each slide, you talk about it as if it's come from the mover's new location. For example, if you take a picture of your local jail, call it ". . . the sumptuous new office building where Gary Woodrell will be taking on his new responsibilities as chief engineer." As you light up a shot of your local bar, present it as ". . . the newly built Skunk's Hollow country club." Maybe you can find a good close-up of your local dump site and tell your guests about ". . . the luxurious and prestigious neighborhood."

Where the Heck Is Hackensack?

This is a game everyone should enjoy, whether they're headed there or not. But it will take a little research on your part.

Go to the library and find a few books on the mover's destination. Dig out thirty to forty obscure facts about the area and jot them down on a piece of paper.

At game time, read the questions aloud and give everyone a chance to write down the answers. For example:

1. "What's New Jersey's nickname?"
2. "The New Jersey state insect is the (a) bumblebee, (b) honeybee, (c) killer bee."

131

3. "What is the title of the New Jersey state song? (a) "Born to Lose," (b) "Itsy-Bitsy, Teeny-Weeny, Yellow Polka Dot Bikini," (c) "Theme from 60 Minutes," (d) None."

4. "Which state boasts the births of Lou Costello, John Forsythe, and Ozzie Nelson—California or New Jersey?"

Read over the answers and tally the score. The winner gets something from the gift suggestion section. You're bound to get a few off-the-wall answers, which makes it all the better.

Geography Class

This game takes us back a few years to our fifth grade assignment. Remove the map hanging on the wall. Distribute paper and pencils to the group and ask them to draw the outline of the mover's new state. Ask them to pinpoint the destination. Give them only five minutes to make the map. Hold up each picture to the group, then take a vote on the best rendering. Award an appropriate prize.

Two additional game ideas are:

● Go around and have each guest tell about his or her best—and *worst*—vacation.

● Have the guests of honor open their "Survival Kits" (see Prizes/Gifts/Favors page 136.)

REFRESHMENTS

Moving Away

● With a "Movable Feast," everyone participates. Decide on how many courses and homes you want to use, then assign them in geographical order, to make "moving" time minimal. You might use a couple of vans to haul the gang around in, so you can keep the party going on the ride in between. Four sites and four courses seem to work best.

Begin with hors d'oeuvres and drinks at one home, and place your "map" there. Ask everyone to bring along a munchy to share.

• Move along to the next house for soup and/or salad. Ask each guest to bring something to toss into a community salad—shredded carrots, bell pepper bits, mushrooms, shredded cheese, croutons, and so on. Ask them also to bring a favorite dressing. You provide a large bowl of red leaf and romaine lettuces. Place all ingredients around the lettuce bowl and let guests serve themselves from the salad bar.

• At the third house comes the entrée. Serve your favorite company dish, or offer this easy-to-make Pesto Linguine.

2 cups fresh basil	2 tablespoons grated
½ cup olive oil	Romano cheese
¼ cup chopped pine nuts	2 pounds fresh linguine
or walnuts	3 tablespoons butter or
½ cup grated fresh	margarine, melted
Parmesan cheese	2 tablespoons water

Place fresh basil in blender with olive oil and nuts. Whirl on high until blended. Pour into bowl, stir in Parmesan and Romano cheeses. Cook fresh linguine in rapidly boiling water for 3 minutes. Drain and place in bowl. Add melted butter and water to pesto; stir into linguine. Serve immediately.

• Finally, wrap up the "Movable Feast" at the last home. Ask each guest to bring along something to dip in the chocolate fondue—apples, mini-marshmallows, nuts, caramels, bananas, peaches, and so on. You provide the chocolate fondue. Melt 8 squares of semisweet baking chocolate and 1 tablespoon butter in saucepan over water or in a microwave. Pour into serving dish with cut-up fruit, etc., on a large platter.

• And if that's not enough food, bake a cake in the shape

of the mover's new state, and decorate it with assorted lakes, rivers, mountains, earthquakes, volcanoes, quicksand, and so on.

Housewarming

• Assign your potluck dishes and tell everyone what to bring (see page 66). If it's a brunch, you'll need drinks (orange juice, Bloody Marys, champagne, coffee), bread (rolls, croissants, pastries, bagels), meat (bacon strips, ham slices, sausage links or patties), and maybe a fruit dish or salad. You may also want to serve a dessert.

• Ask your guests to bring along the recipe with the dish, or to bring the dish in a nice basket, plate, or serving item, to leave with the new homeowners as a gift.

Bon Voyage

• Serve refreshments or a meal that the vacationers might find at their destination. For example, if they're headed for Mexico, have a Mexican fiesta dinner, with margaritas, enchiladas, burritos, tostadas, and flan for dessert. Serve a Polynesian dinner for the tropics, baked Alaska for the Yukon, Irish stew for a culinary visit to Ireland, or sukiyaki for a preview of Japan.

PRIZES/GIFTS/FAVORS

Moving Away

• Have some "I'm not from New Jersey" (or wherever) buttons made up for all the guests to wear.
• If there are any game winners, present them with guidebooks to the new area or state.

- Think about the stereotype of the new area—does it suggest anything for gift ideas? For example: oversized items for Texas, sunglasses for California or the topics, foreign language books for overseas, apples for New York, and so on.
- One gift idea for the movers is stationery—all self-addressed and stamped. It gives them no excuse not to write! Add an address book, too.
- You might wear that T-shirt we mentioned earlier, with another underneath so you can peel it off at the end of the party and present it to the relocating guests.
- Give the movers some local wines to help them remember the gang and forget their sorrows.
- Have a nice photograph of the old house taken, or hire an artist to draw a picture of it; have it framed and give it as a gift to the movers.
- Give the movers a one-year subscription to your local newspaper to help ease the transition.

Housewarming

- Have your guests contribute to a household tree. Make a wooden tree from scrap lumber, then tie on much-needed

tools for new owners—hammer, screwdriver, plunger, and so on.

• Ask everyone to bring a plant as, or with, their gift.

• Ask everyone to bring a sample from a favorite store (see centerpiece, page 129).

• Ask all your guests to bring a frozen meal and present it to the new family at the party. They'll have a stock of dinners to last until they get settled.

Travelers

• Make up a "Survival Kit" for the travelers, with such items as plug adapters, Dramamine, foreign language phrase book, self-addressed-stamped postcards already filled in, maps, film, freeze-dried snacks, some foreign currency, and so on.

• Travel and guidebooks would be a welcome gift.

• How about an airplane bag full of things to do on the plane, such as magazines, fruit and nuts, puzzles, small traveling games, a best-selling novel, and so on.

ADULTS-ONLY PARTIES

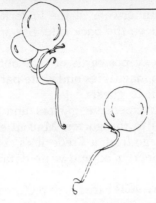

Bachelor and Bachelorette parties are still a tradition for many soon-to-be-married people. While the Bachelor party for the men is less formal, the Bachelorette party gives the women an opportunity to get a bit wicked. Many women take the opportunity to visit a male strip joint, such as Chippendales, or they get together and hire a male stripper to "drop in" during the course of the party. They usually arrive in some kind of costume—such as a cowboy getup or a police uniform—switch on a cassette player, and start dancing as they peel off their clothes (usually they leave on a G-string or bikini underwear). You can find them in the Yellow Pages under "Entertainers."

You could also make your Bachelorette party a lingerie party—ask your guests to come in sexy nightwear and have a lingerie hostess come to the party to show the latest styles. (You might want to ask the men to this party, too, and it's fun if they've dressed in black tie.)

As for how to throw a Bachelor party—well, it couldn't be easier. Read on. . . .

INVITATIONS

Bachelorette

- Buy paper underwear at the lingerie store and write your party details on the back side. Slip into envelope and mail to guests.
- Buy some sexy postcards or tear out a few sexy pictures of men from magazines and write party information in clear spaces. Mail to guests.
- Buy some inexpensive garters and tie a card with party information to the garter. Mail in envelope.
- Tear out a page from a Frederick's of Hollywood catalog or Victoria's Secrets ad and write details of party. Mail to guests.
- The card store sells cards with pictures of the Chippendale male strippers—perfect for using as an invitation.
- If you're hosting a lingerie party, ask your guests to wear sexy lingerie.

Bachelor Party

- Phone them. . . .

DECORATIONS

Bachelorette

- Buy a couple of *Playgirl* magazines and tape the foldouts to the walls.
- Buy some posters of popular hunks—preferably with their shirts off—and tape them to the walls. You can use these as prizes for the game winners, too.

- Make a basket of items for the honeymoon night—cologne, breath spray, body paint, sexy panties, a sex manual—and tie it with a white ribbon to use as a centerpiece. Give the basket to the bride-to-be as your gift.
- Buy two postcards each of several different hunks. Place one at each place setting. Place the others in a sewn-up pair of jockey shorts (or a bag) and let each guest pick her hunk from the bag. She then has to match her hunk card to the card on the table to determine where she sits.

Bachelor

- All the decorating you need to do is switch on the TV and VCR. . . .

GAMES/ACTIVITIES

Bachelorette

- If you hire a male stripper, plan for him to come near the end of the party, to ensure that all the guests will be there. You'll definitely want to keep his visit a secret from the bride-to-be, but you may also want to keep your other guests in the dark, too, so he surprises everyone!
- Place items that are primarily associated with men in doubled lunch bags. You might include such things as a can of shaving cream, jockey shorts, a popular men's cologne, a little black book, and a condom. Have each of the guests feel what's inside the bag and write down their answers. The one with the most correct answers wins a prize (maybe something from one of the bags).
- Buy a large poster of the bride's favorite hunk. A full-body shot would be best. With paper and pencil, trace your favorite body part, outline it in black felt pen, and pho-

tocopy it for your guests. At game time, have them play "Pin the (body part) on the Hunk."

• Pick out some words from the dictionary that sound a little risqué but aren't necessarily. Pass out paper and pencil for "Sex Education." Read your pre-chosen words and have your guests make up definitions for each word. Then have them all read their definitions aloud. If anyone gets the word right, she gets a point, but most of the answers will probably be funny. A few words to get you started—fug (a bad smell), dastard (coward), dik-dik (African antelope), sextant (a measuring instrument), titivate (to make smart).

Bachelor

• Switch on the movie. . . .

REFRESHMENTS

Bachelorette

Most Bachelorette parties are held in the evening, with just drinks, snacks, and desserts. Here are a few suggestions:

• Fill cream puffs with pistachio ice cream and top with caramel sauce.
• Layer parfait glasses with mint-chocolate chip ice cream and graham cracker crumbs. Top with whipped cream and a sprinkling of mini chocolate chips.
• Serve a berry whip by blending 1 cup strawberries, 1 cup plain yogurt, 1 tablespoon lemon juice, and 2 teaspoons honey in the blender.
• See Wedding Shower (page 18) for more ideas on refreshments.
• Tell your guests all your refreshments are aphrodisiacs.

Bachelor

- Just make sure there's plenty of beer and pretzels. . . .

PRIZES/GIFTS/FAVORS

Bachelorette

- For prizes, give the winners a sexy book or magazine, some sexy underwear, or some of the items in the men's bags.
- If your guests need gift ideas, suggest a padded bra, sexy lingerie or underwear, a nice cologne, a sex manual.
- If you want to give your guests favors, how about those items in the bags, lingerie catalogs, paper underwear.
- Bride's First-Aid Kit—jar of vaseline, toilet paper, phony birth control pills, cherry douche, back-scrub brush, bubble bath, cheap champagne, tabloid newspaper, romance novel, bonbons, headache pills, nail file, and so on.

Bachelor

- Are you kidding? Maybe a couple of Alka Seltzer. . . .

MORE EXCUSES FOR A PARTY

Still need more excuses for a party? Here are some quick ideas for further celebration:

"M*A*S*H" Bash

Have your guests come dressed as characters from the long-running television show—medical outfits, military uniforms, or just Hawaiian shirts. Hang pictures from the TV show around the house, decorate the party room as Rosie's Bar, serve food in a chow line with old TV trays.

Charade Party

Have the gang over for an evening of charades. Make it a particular theme—horror movies, TV shows, children's books—and have them either play the official way, breaking sentences into words and syllables, or have them act out scenes.

Treasure Hunt

Write clues and place them around the house, the neighborhood, or the city. Assign couples or teams and send them out on foot or by car. Have each clue a cryptic message so it's not too easy to follow, and have alternate directions if they make a wrong guess!

Roaring Twenties

Dress in costume and have rooms set up with different gambling games going on in each one—roulette, cards, and so on. Have one room just for music from the twenties and let everyone dance.

International Evening

Ask your guests to come dressed in costumes of their heritage or as their favorite foreigner. Have them bring dishes representative of that region and some interesting facts, games, or other items to share with the group.

Toga Party

Ask your guests to come in Roman togas. Send out invitations on small parchment scrolls, serve Greek food, drink wine from goblets, play the "Drop the Grape into Caesar's Mouth" game.

Murder Mystery Party

Buy one of the murder mystery party books or games available, such as *Secret of the Bitter Sweets, Greetings from the Grave,* or *Deadly Game of Klew,* by Penny and Tom Warner (St. Martin's Press, 1986), and have your friends over to solve the mystery. Or host a large party with eight friends playing the role of suspects, and have the rest be the sleuths. Ask the extra guests to come dressed as their favorite detective (or villain).

Clambake

Have a clambake at the beach or in the backyard. You might also serve a shrimp cocktail, have a crab feed, or an abalone feast.

Gone with the Wind *Garden Party*

Turn your backyard into a Southern garden, with flowers, ribbons and bows, balloons, and so on. Ask your guests to dress as Southern belles in formal sundresses and formal-wear. Have the party served by teenagers, rent tents and umbrellas, and play croquet. Hang pictures of Scarlett O'Hara and Rhett Butler and play some GWTW trivia.

Texas Barbecue

Have everyone dress as cowboys and cowgirls, in jeans, checked shirts, and string ties. Barbecue ribs on the grills, have a hoedown and square dance with a real caller, and arrange for a hayride in the country.

Cinco de Mayo

Serve Mexican food—margaritas, fajitas, guacamole, nachos. Ask your guests to dress in serapes, peasant blouses, ponchos, sombreros, and so on. Set the stage with colorful items from Mexico—paper flowers, Christmas lights, piñatas, and so on.

Soup Group

Get the gang together on a regular basis and try out a new soup each time. Serve salad and bread with it and plan an activity, such as "How Did You Meet?" charades, cards, Trivial Pursuit, and so on.

Victim of Fashion Party

Ever buy something you regretted but never threw away because it was (a) so expensive, (b) a gift from someone, (c) something you *had* to have, (d) such a bargain. Well you're not alone. Now's the time to host a Victim of Fashion Party. Ask your friends to come dressed in a similar outfit and spend the evening laughing and sharing stories about it. Maybe end with a trade or auction.

Taste of America Party

Have each guest or group of guests set up tables with different city themes, such as San Francisco with a toy cable car, flowers, and sourdough bread. Have each table assigned to a part of the meal—appetizers, salads, soups, main course, desserts, drinks. The San Francisco table

could feature sourdough bread with the appetizer, crab cocktails for the salad, artichoke bisque for soup, sukiyaki for main course, orange mousse for dessert, or California coolers for the drinks. Have each group dress in typical attire from the area.

Ski Party

You don't have to have snow to have a ski party. Just have your guests dress in snow bunny apparel, set the atmosphere with a nice fire, a few resort names on the walls, and a centerpiece made from goggles, ski wax, and a pair of broken skis. Serve stew or chili and hot drinks. Talk about skiing!

Mother/Daughter Tea

No matter how old your daughter is, she's just the right age for a mother/daughter tea. Have several mothers and daughters over for a luncheon or snack. Have your daughter help with preparation. Make it a dress up, or have mom dress like daughter and daughter dress like mom. Make it a cookie exchange or a make-your-own sundae event. Have all the guests take turns answering some relevant questions—"What's most important in our friendship?" "What I like about my mom (daughter)." "What we'll be doing in five (ten, and so on) years."

Lottery Party

Have your friends come with a certain number of lottery tickets. Scratch the tickets with a slow buildup. Award any winners with a turn at the big spin for a wrapped prize—a book on how to stop gambling, ten more lottery tickets, a book on contests.

Mortgage Payoff Party

The mortgage payoff is a big event in everyone's life—a perfect time to celebrate. Bring the lucky people joke gifts like brochures for a cruise, new house ads, bank account promos, and so on.

Income Tax Party

April 15 is the day to hold your Income Tax Party. Set the table with old newspapers and plain paper plates. Mail invitations on IRS forms. Ask your guests to wear rags.

Tacky Party

Have all your guests dress their tackiest—taped glasses, plaid pants with a print shirt, and so on. Ask them to bring a tacky gift to exchange. Serve tacky food—American cheese sandwiches, chocolate milk, Fig Newtons for dessert. Play tacky games—Musical Chairs, Bingo, Go Fish, Spin the Bottle, Simon Says.

Invite a Friend Party

At your next gathering have each member of your group invite a new couple. It's a great way to meet new people.

INDEX

If you enjoyed *Penny Warner's Party Book,* you will also enjoy her other party books:

Happy Birthday Parties!: Over twenty unique and creative party ideas—including a dinosaur party, star invaders party, storybook party, beauty salon party, Acapulco Olé—guaranteed to turn your child's birthday into a special and memorable occasion. Includes ideas for invitations, decorations, games, plus recipes for cakes and refreshments.

Murder Mystery Party books, by Penny and Tom Warner: Now you can throw witty, exciting mystery parties in your own home. "Suspects" are instructed to dress and act in character, follow an individual script, and move through the maze of clues in search of the murderer. Each book includes complete instructions, invitations, name tags, aliases, scripts, alibis, clues, and, of course, the Hidden Solution.

Now available:

A Deadly Game of Klew, for six players
Greetings from the Grave, for eight players
The Secret of the Bitter Sweets, for eight players

Happy Birthday Parties!, A Deadly Game of Klew, Greetings from the Grave, and *The Secret of the Bitter Sweets* are available at your local bookstore, or you can order them directly from the publisher by returning this coupon with check or money order to St. Martin's Press, 175 Fifth Avenue, New York, N.Y., 10010, Attn: Cash Sales. For information on credit card orders, quantity orders, and discounts, call the St. Martin's Press Special Sales Dept. toll-free at (800) 221-7945. In New York State, call (212) 674-5151.

Please send me _____ copy(ies) of **HAPPY BIRTHDAY PARTIES!**
(ISBN 0-312-36180-7) @ $9.95 per book $_____

Please send me _____ copy(ies) of **A DEADLY GAME OF KLEW**
(ISBN 0-312-70857-2) @ $7.95 per book $_____

Please send me _____ copy(ies) of **GREETINGS FROM THE
GRAVE**
(ISBN 0-312-18527-8) @ $7.95 per book $_____

Please send me _____ copy(ies) of **THE SECRET OF THE BITTER
SWEETS**
(ISBN 0-312-35029-5) @ $7.95 per book $_____

Postage and handling

($1.50 for first copy + $.75 for each additional) $_____

Amount enclosed $_____

Name _____

Organization _____

Address _____

City _____

State _____ Zip _____